The Sforza Castle in Milan

Marsilio

1. p. 18
Umberto I or Filarete Tower
2. p. 24
Santo Spirito Gate
3. p. 24
Carmine Gate
4.
Barcho Gate
5. p. 20
Santo Spirito Tower
6. p. 20
Carmine Tower
7. p. 26
Castellana Tower
8. p. 29
Falconiera Tower
9. p. 24
Cortile delle Armi
10. p. 26
Cortile della Rocchetta
11. p. 29
Corte Ducale
12. p. 24
Porta Giovia
13. p. 26
Bona of Savoy Tower
14. p. 29
Portico dell'Elefante
15. p. 29
Loggetta di Galeazzo Maria
16. p. 20
Rivellino of Santo Spirito
17.
Panoramic Halls*

18.
Visconti Halls*
19. p. 29
Treasury Hall*
20.
Castellana Hall*
21. p. 24
Spanish Hospital Halls*
22. p. 29
Ponticella
23. p. 32-36
Spanish Hospital
24. p. 22
Covered Road of the Ghirlanda
25. p. 18
Battlements
26. Starting Point
for Guided Tours
27. p. 22
Dead Moat
28. p. 22
Outer Moats

*Temporary Exhibitions

- Info point
- Museum Security
- Ticket Office
- Nursery
- Cloakroom
- Audio Guides
- Bookshop
- Café
- Toilets

1. p. 32
The *Pietà Rondanini* Museum-Michelangelo
2. p. 38
The Museum of Ancient Art
3. p. 54
The Sala delle Asse
4. p. 58
The Museum of Furniture
and Wooden Sculptures
5. p. 66
The Picture Gallery
6. p. 76
The Museum of Decorative Arts
7. p. 84
The Museum of Musical Instruments
8. p. 92
The Museum of Archaeology
The Prehistory and Protohistory Section
9. p. 96
The Museum of Archaeology
The Egyptian Section

Castle Attractions and Museums

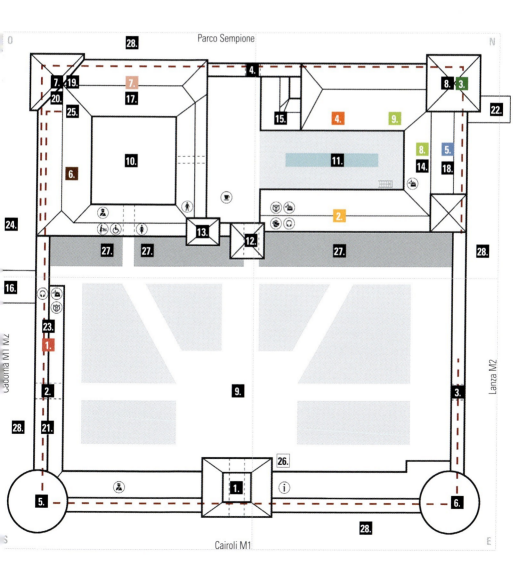

Texts
Maria Teresa Donati, Nicoletta Sfredda with Thea Tibiletti

Photographs
The photographic campaign was curated
by Roberto Mascaroni, except for the photo
on page 107 by Gianluca Di Ioia – La Triennale di Milano,
the photos on pp. 105, 106 and 108
by Nicoletta Sfredda – Nuova Chorós,
and the photo on pp. 6-7 © marcoemilia, Fotolia

Translation
Sylvia Notini

Cover
Filarete or Umberto I Tower

Editing and layout
Maria Giulia Montessori

© Comune di Milano 2016

Editorial realization by
Marsilio Editori® s.p.a.
in Venice
First edition May 2016
ISBN 88-317-2569-9
www.marsilioeditori.it

CONTENTS

10 From the Visconti to Our Day. The History of a Grand Building

16 The Castle Today
18 Echoes of the Past: Outside Defense
24 Inside the Castle

30 The Castle Museums
32 The *Pietà Rondanini* Museum-Michelangelo
38 The Museum of Ancient Art
54 The Sala delle Asse (Room VIII)
58 The Museum of Furniture and Wooden Sculptures
66 The Picture Gallery
76 The Museum of Decorative Arts
84 The Museum of Musical Instruments
92 The Museum of Archaeology. The Prehistory and Protohistory Section
96 The Museum of Archaeology. The Egyptian Section

102 The Cultural Institutes of the Sforza Castle
104 Parco Sempione

111 Essential References

From the Visconti to Our Day.
The History of a Grand Building

The Visconti and Porta Giovia Fortress
Between 1360 and 1370 Galeazzo II Visconti, who shared the government of Milan with his brother Bernabò, had a square fortress built straddling the medieval city walls. This new fortification encompassed the Pusterla Giovia (from *posterula*, small door), from which it got its name. In 1392 Gian Galeazzo, his son, had a citadel for the troops under his command built adjoining the first structure. The Visconti fortalice, made up of two parts that were still separated by the ancient moat of medieval Milan (the so-called "dead moat"), featured a plan that was rather similar to that of the contemporary Pavia Castle, and it was decided it would be used as a fortress and a prison. It was not until the period of the last Visconti, Filippo Maria, that the Castle took on the guise of a seigneurial residence. He connected the two parts that were separated by the moat and had a large park created northwards, spending his solitary life in this vast residence.

After the Visconti
In 1447 Filippo Maria Visconti died leaving no legitimate male heirs. His daughter Bianca Maria was legitimized in 1426 by Emperor Sigismund to succeed her father's estate, but not to inherit the ducal title. Bianca would nevertheless play a major role in the city of Milan. In 1441 she had married the military leader Francesco Sforza, summoned by Visconti to defend the Duchy of Milan from the Venetians. When Filippo Maria died, the citizens proclaimed the Ambrosian Republic. In that period the Duke's residence was damaged and partially demolished. The stones taken from the Castle were used to pay off creditors and restore the city walls.

The Sforza
An experienced soldier and clever politician, Francesco Sforza changed sides more than once, in the end subjecting Milan to a bitter siege. His determination led to his being welcomed with Bianca Maria Visconti on 26 March 1450 as lord of the city. It was the start of a peaceful period for Milan. The Castle was restored and endowed with an elegant entrance on the city side, designed by the Tuscan architect Antonio Averulino, called Il Filarete. On the same side two round

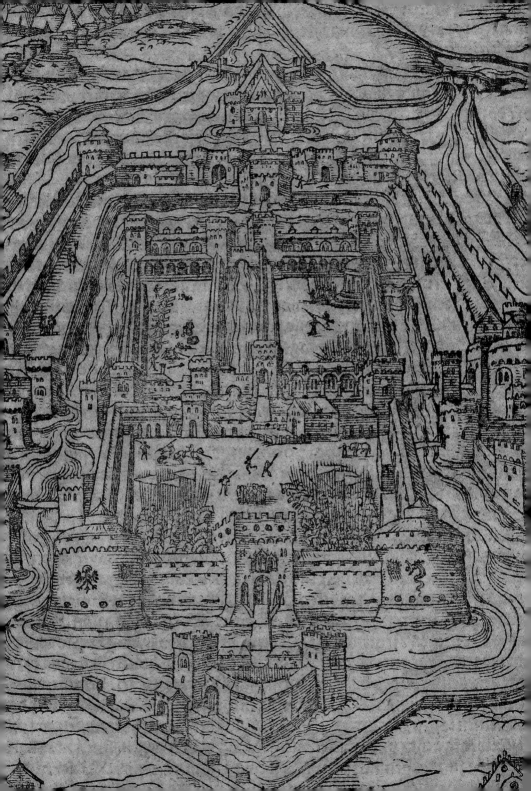

Portraits of Francesco Sforza and Bianca Maria Visconti on the portal of the Banco Mediceo, ca. 1464, Candoglia marble, Museum of Ancient Art, Room XIV (Armory)

previous page
View of the Sforza Castle, detail, ca. 1552-1588, woodcut, Milan, Civica Raccolta delle Stampe "Achille Bertarelli"

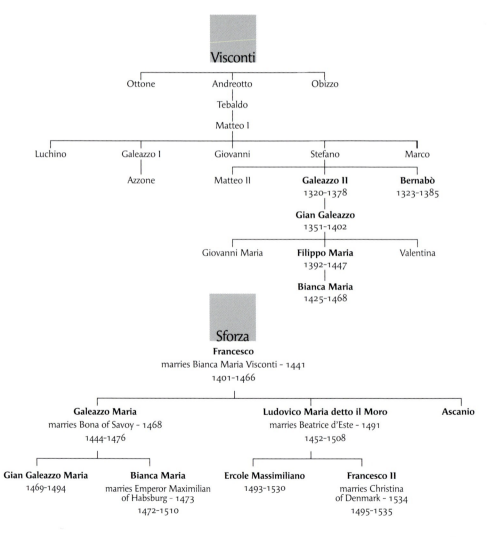

FROM THE VISCONTI TO OUR DAY

right
Francesco Napoletano, *Madonna Lia*, detail, ca. 1490, oil on canvas.
In the background view of the Filarete Tower and the ravelin facing the city side entrance

towers were erected and clad in diamond-shaped serizzo stone, more suited to defending the Castle from enemy artillery. Like the round towers, the expansion of the Ghirlanda, a walled curtain that had already existed in the Visconti era, whose purpose was to defend the northern side, is the work of the military engineer Bartolomeo Gadio. Francesco Sforza and his consort never lived in the newly restored Castle, which in 1468 instead became the home of Galeazzo Maria, who had succeeded his father two years earlier, and his wife Bona of Savoy, the sister-in-law of the French king Louis XI. In those years of intense activity, overseen by the loyal Gadio and the Tuscan architect Benedetto Ferrini, the Rocchetta and the Corte Ducale were completed, overlooked by the apartments of the lords of Milan, with spacious frescoed rooms. In just one year, 1473, the Ducal Chapel was built and frescoed; it is now Room XII of the Museum of Ancient Art. In 1476 thirty-two-old Galeazzo Maria was murdered in a plot. He was succeeded by his young heir, Gian Galeazzo Maria, under the regency of his mother Bona. Remaining today in the Castle in memory of Bona is the tall tower in the Rocchetta, built to better guard over the entire building. Soon afterwards, however, Milan's fate would be determined by the rise to power of Ludovico il Moro, the brother of the lord who had been murdered. Ludovico gave the city a period of peace, and he commissioned artists of the caliber of Donato Bramante and Leonardo da Vinci to beautify it. Ludovico was the only Sforza to be awarded the ducal investiture by the emperor in 1495, but this was still not enough to preserve his power. Forced to flee when Louis XII arrived in Milan in 1499, advancing claims upon the Duchy, Ludovico, after returning briefly to the city, died a prisoner in Loche Castle, France, in 1508.

From Residence to Barracks
In this complex period, during which the Duchy of Milan was fought over by the Sforza, the French king, and the German emperor, the Castle, a crucial point of the city to be conquered, found itself at the heart of conflicts and attacks. In two decades (1515-1534), the French domination of Francis I d'Angoulême, successor to Louis XII, was followed by the short-lived rule of Francis II Sforza, Ludovico's second-born son, and after that by a short-lived Spanish government, which ended with Sforza's return, who in 1535 left emperor Charles V as heir to the Duchy.

Grey serizzo stone talus from the Visconti period, on the Castle facade facing the Parco Sempione

below
Giovanni Antolini, *Plan for the Foro Bonaparte*, 1801, etching, Milan, Civica Raccolta delle Stampe "Achille Bertarelli"

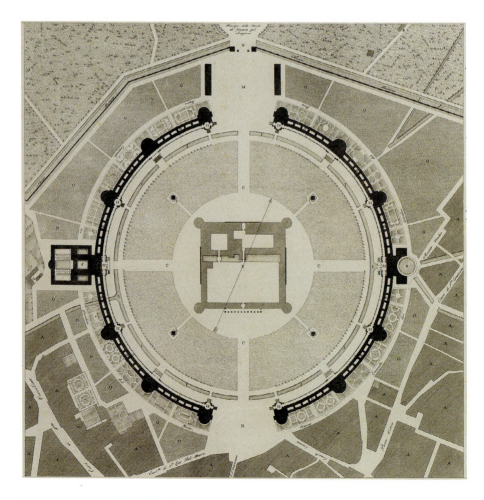

FROM THE VISCONTI TO OUR DAY

In 1521, under French rule, the Filarete Tower, used to store gunpowder, exploded, damaging the ancient building's walls. Restored to host the marriage between Francis II Sforza and Christina of Denmark on 3 June 1534, immediately afterwards the Castle would never again be a noble residence.

Traces of Foreign Domination
Having become the seat of the Spanish garrison, the building hosted about 2,000 soldiers, and included a hospital, apothecary, shops, bakery, two ovens, a tavern, a "nevera" to preserve ice. The imposing framework of fortifications undertaken in 1549 by Ferrante Gonzaga, captain general and lieutenant of the emperor, defended the castle with a twelve-pointed star-shaped wall. Witness to the Spanish period, besides the hospital – which in May 2015 became the *Pietà Rondanini* Museum-Michelangelo – is the painted decoration of three rooms now part of the Museum of Ancient Art, decorated on the occasion of the marriage in 1554 between the Duke of Milan Philip of Habsburg, future King Philip II, and his cousin Mary Tudor, Queen of England and Ireland. The passing of the years did not change the Castle's use. During the War of the Spanish Succession, in 1706, Eugene of Savoy conquered Milan on behalf of Emperor Joseph I of Habsburg. The only trace of this period is the marble statue of Saint John of Nepomuk in the Cortile delle Armi, near the entrance to the Corte Ducale. Dedicated to the patron saint of Bohemian armies, the commander Annibale Visconti commissioned it from the sculptor Giovanni Dugnani in 1727. In 1796, as Napoleon Bonaparte approached and after the city was abandoned by Archduke Ferdinand I of Austria, a mob of Milanese citizens who were French sympathizers tried to attack the much-hated fortress that had for so long been occupied by the invaders, in a sort of tribute to the Storming of the Bastille. The citizens were, however, driven back by the Austrian garrison under the orders of General Lamy. During the subsequent French domination the star-shaped fortress was dismantled and a huge circular space was designed, the Foro Bonaparte; as for the Castle, a new classical form was conceived, to be preceded by an atrium featuring a colonnade. When the Austrians returned in 1815, the only thing that changed for the building was the soldiers' provenance. The site from which General Radetzky bombed the city during the Five Days (18-22 March 1848), the round towers of the fortress were lowered by the Milanese, and it was substantially devastated by the citizens themselves when Austrian rule finally came to an end in 1859.

A New Use for the Castle
Perceived as being a place that was closed to the city, and a post from which Milan had to defend itself over the course of the centuries, the Castle was saved from demolition thanks to the commitment of the Milanese citizens and Luca Beltrami, the architect who devoted many years of his life to rescuing and restoring the building, starting in 1892. Convinced that his task was to restore the fortress to its former glories during the Sforza era, Beltrami promoted the many projects that transformed the Castle into what it is today, re-excavating the moats and rebuilding, according to the iconographic and historical sources, the Filarete Tower, dedicated to King Umberto I and inaugurated on 24 September 1905. In its role as a citadel of art and culture, since the early 20th century the Castle has hosted exceptional institutions and museums.

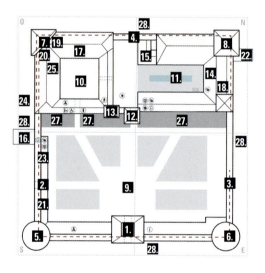

1. Umberto I or Filarete Tower
2. Santo Spirito Gate
3. Carmine Gate
4. Barcho Gate
5. Santo Spirito Tower
6. Carmine Tower
7. Castellana Tower
8. Falconiera Tower
9. Cortile delle Armi
10. Cortile della Rocchetta
11. Corte Ducale
12. Porta Giovia
13. Bona of Savoy Tower
14. Portico dell'Elefante
15. Loggetta di Galeazzo Maria
16. Rivellino of Santo Spirito
17. Panoramic Halls
18. Visconti Halls
19. Treasury Hall
20. Castellana Hall
21. Spanish Hospital Halls
22. Ponticella
23. Spanish Hospital
24. Covered Road of the Ghirlanda
25. Battlements
27. Dead Moat
28. Outer Moats

The Castle Today

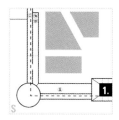

The Castle we find before us today, stripped of all the stratifications and transformations it underwent over centuries of foreign rule, is the result of a large-scale restoration begun in 1893 by the architect Luca Beltrami; to bestow the ancient manor with its original 15th-century appearance, he reconstructed or reintegrated, based on meticulous documentary research, many of its parts, including the battlements and wall-walks.

Echoes of the Past: Outside Defense

1. The Filarete or Umberto I Tower
The tall central tower overlooking the main entrance to the Castle was completely designed by Beltrami. Unfortunately, the original tower was short-lived. Built in 1452 to a design by the Tuscan architect Antonio Averulino, called Il Filarete (ca. 1400 – ca. 1469), it collapsed less than a century later, on 28 June 1521 while under French rule, when the gunpowder stored inside it exploded. Beltrami, in order to reconstruct its original form, meticulously researched the documents and iconographic sources. Particularly helpful were a painting by the school of Leonardo, now in the Sforza Castle – the *Madonna Lia* by Francesco Napoletano (ca. 1490), where one can glimpse the tower – and a graffito discovered in the Pozzobonelli farmhouse nearby. On the facade of the tower facing the city one can see the decorations that Beltrami chose to add to it: a clock with the Sforza motif of a sun with rays, the coats of arms of the great members of the Sforza house, and a 14th-century-style statue of Saint Ambrose, patron saint of Milan, which the architect commissioned, together with a Candoglia marble bas-relief of Umberto I on horseback, from the sculptor Luigi Secchi (1853-1921).
The tower, thus reconstructed and dedicated to Umberto I King of Italy, shot dead in Monza on 29 July 1900, was solemnly inaugurated on 24 September 1905.

1.

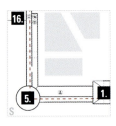

16.

5. The Santo Spirito and Carmine Towers

Rising up on either end of the Castle facade facing the city are the imposing Santo Spirito Tower, to the left, and the Carmine Tower, to the right, which Francesco Sforza had built to improve the Castle's defenses and power to withstand the new enemy weapons.

These low cylindrical corner towers, a novelty in the field of military architecture, featured walls that were 7 metres thick and clad in diamond-shaped serizzo stone, giving them a less austere and rather unique shape. Precisely because of their original appearance the towers were appreciated and often recalled, as the documents report, by visitors and ambassadors from the Sforza period. The interior consisted of six rooms placed one atop the other, covered with vaults and illuminated through embrasures. In the 16th century and again in 1848, during Milan's uprising against the Austrians, the towers were lowered. Their current appearance is due to the work of Luca Beltrami, who restored their original height in the late 19th century.

16. The Ravelins

Visible along the outside of the Castle are the remains of the "ravelins", military posts built to intercept the enemy, defend the castle from invasion, and watch over the moat. The architects commissioned by Francesco Sforza to restructure the fortilice included in their renovation the construction of these outposts around 1455, which may already have existed in the Visconti era. Of the various Sforza ravelins that protected the Castle, still visible today inside the outer moat are some foundations and a single structure with part of the elevation, the Rivellino di Santo Spirito (facing today's Piazza Cadorna). Its current appearance, however, is the result of the efforts of Luca Beltrami who, between 1911 and 1914, restored part of the battlements that had been demolished under Spanish rule, along with the interiors.

In the late 15th century, in order to keep up with the rapidly-changing innovations in offensive techniques, Ludovico il Moro commissioned Leonardo to design a ravelin in the new pentagonal shape; however, this was made later, when Milan was already under the French rule of Louis XII, between 1499 and early 1500. The very few traces left of this bulwark can be seen under the cobbled surface in front of the main entrance.

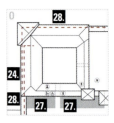

24. The Ghirlanda and the Covered Road

Still circling the outside of the Castle, along the rear, where the park begins, visitors will find the remains of the Colubrina Tower, the Vittoria Tower, and of an entrance door, the Porta del Soccorso, the sole remains of another defensive structure for the Castle: the Ghirlanda, an encircling wall that already existed under Visconti rule, and that was repaired and extended under Francesco Sforza. The Ghirlanda, featuring two round corner towers, crowned the Castle outside, from the Rivellino of Santo Spirito in a south-westerly direction, towards that of the Carmine to the north-east; it was also surrounded by a moat, where the waters of the Naviglio flowed together. The ravelins served as a link between these walls and the Castle via drawbridges. A drawing by Leonardo, dated to between 1487 and 1490, in manuscript B (Paris, Institut de France), shows a section of the Ghirlanda and of the Castle in the north-western corner with all the dimensions of the fortress. During the restoration work in 1893 most of the Ghirlanda was demolished, but the covered road survived.

The covered road, located in the counterscarp of the moat around the Castle, thanks to its many trails, allowed the soldiers to move from the fortress to the Ghirlanda without being seen from the Castle. Visitors can take a walk through this tunnel accompanied by a guide; the portion that survived the demolition in the late 19th century was restored.

The tunnel was made of bricks, with a vaulted ceiling 2.80 m high; it was lit by about one hundred small windows overlooking the moat, from which sharpshooters could take aim.

27. 28. The Moats

Among the defensive works built to stave off enemies and make the fortress safer there simply had to be a moat. The moat around the Castle, attributed to the period when Francesco Sforza (1450-1466) ruled, was buried in the 17th century and disinterred between the late 19th and early 20th centuries.

Located inside the building, in the Cortile delle Armi, is the ancient moat, the so-called "dead moat", excavated to defend Milan's medieval walls on top of which the castle was built during the Visconti period.

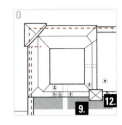

Inside the Castle

The Castle comprises two structures separated by the dead moat: on this side of the moat the Cortile delle Armi was developed; located on the other side are the Rocchetta and the Corte Ducale.

9. The Cortile delle Armi

Upon entering the Castle from the Filarete Tower visitors will find the Cortile delle Armi, a vast rectangular courtyard, extensively restored by Luca Beltrami. On the left-hand side of the courtyard, facing the Santo Spirito Gate, is a quarter that was erected under Spanish domination, which included several shops, an apothecary, and a hospital; this became the *Pietà Rondanini* Museum-Michelangelo in 2015. The right-hand side, towards the Carmine Gate, also known as Carmineto, hosts Late Roman stone sarcophaguses (3rd-4th century), fragments of statues, and the architectural remains of Milanese buildings dated from the Middle Ages to the 17th century. These were collected in the early 20th century by Luca Beltrami to create a small open-air museum. Also rebuilt against the walled curtain was the Renaissance facade of Palazzo Landriani's portico, and the facade facing the inner courtyard in one of the buildings in Via Spadari.

12. Porta Giovia

The Cortile delle Armi leads to the Corte Ducale and to the Rocchetta through an entrance set in the site occupied by Porta Giovia in the city's medieval walls, on which the Visconti castle was built. During the period when Luca Beltrami was refurbishing the Castle, in the late 19th century, the passage was decorated with a fresco representing a *Crucifixion and Saints*, commissioned between 1470 and 1480 by Ambrosino di Longhignana, captain general of the infantry of the Castle guards. Only the sinopia of the fresco, which was detached in 1969 and moved to the Pinacoteca (Picture Gallery), is known of today. On display to the left of the atrium are terracotta decorative elements from a window sill and moulding dated to the last two decades of the 15th century. Visible on the same side, above, are the remains of a headless stone bust of a bishop, dated to between the 12th and the 13th centuries, and four large female heads that in the late 16th century decorated the attic of Palaz-

12. 13.

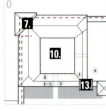

zo Marino. In the 1980s several fragments from large-scale Candoglia marble sculptures were placed on the wall in front: the head of God the Father and a cherubim, an angel and a male head from the late 15th century, ascribed to Martino Benzoni or his collaborators, and perhaps originally from the facade of the ancient church of Santa Maria Annunciata, which was demolished in order to enlarge the Castle when Francesco Sforza was in power. Visible outside, facing the Corte Ducale, is the 16th-century commemorative stone of the poet Ausonius.

13. The Bona of Savoy Tower and the Rocchetta

At the far end of the Cortile delle Armi, to the left, are the Rocchetta, the first structure to be built during the Visconti age, and the Bona of Savoy Tower, which was built, as we are told by the name, by Bona of Savoy. When the lord of Milan Galeazzo Maria (son of Francesco Sforza and Bianca Maria Visconti) was stabbed during a conspiracy on 26 December 1476, his wife Bona took refuge in the Rocchetta, a stronghold with no openings; she later had a tall rectangular tower added so that the entire Castle could be watched over. Damaged during foreign rule, Beltrami had the tower raised and battlements added during the Castle's late 19th-century restoration.

10. The Cortile della Rocchetta

The Cortile delle Armi leads into the Cortile della Rocchetta, at one time accessible only via a drawbridge. Endowed with a sole portico with serizzo stone columns on the south-west side while Francesco Sforza was in rule, the courtyard was completed between 1490 and 1495 with the colonnade to the right, towards the Corte Ducale. Emblems from the Sforza era, like the snake, the imperial eagle, the whisk-broom, and the caduceus between two dragons decorate the Corinthian capitals, while coats of arms featuring three half-moons, the emblem of the castellan Don Avaro de Luna, recall the Spanish presence in the city in the 16th century. Restorations between 2010 and 2013 have uncovered the Neo-Renaissance decorations on the portico walls and vaults that Luca Beltrami restored.

7. The Castellana Tower

Francesco Sforza believed that the Castellana Tower was the safest place in the Rocchetta. This is

where the castellan lived. In the Treasury Hall on the ground floor, a fresco commissioned by Ludovico il Moro from Bartolomeo Suardi, called Bramantino (known of from 1480 to 1530), is still visible today: it is a representation of Argo, the mythological one-hundred-eyed giant, the symbolic protector of the Castle treasure.

11. The Corte Ducale

The Corte Ducale is located opposite the Rocchetta; it contained the residences, meeting rooms, and ducal chancellery. Galeazzo Maria, Francesco Sforza's successor, promoted major building and decorative work that gave the Corte Ducale a new appearance, that of a seigneurial residence. In 1470 Galeazzo Maria hired the Tuscan architect Benedetto Ferrini, to whom is especially due the six-arched portico on the eastern side of the courtyard. What has remained of the decoration on the walls is the figure of a large elephant, hence, "Portico dell'Elefante", and traces of a fresco depicting a lion. The ducal apartments, where Galeazzo Maria Sforza lived from 1468, extended as far as the ground and first floors, connected by a staircase with low steps that allowed Sforza to ride his horse all the way up to the apartments at the top. The small loggia on the first floor is the result of Beltrami's extensive restoration.

8. The Falconiera Tower

On the north-eastern corner of the Corte Ducale is a square tower with the Sala delle Asse (Room VIII of the Museum of Ancient Art) on the ground floor, painted by Leonardo da Vinci in 1498.

22. The Ponticella

Adjoining the Sala delle Asse, the Ponticella was a loggia that made it possible to bypass the outer moat. Ludovico il Moro had it built, and it consisted of three small rooms overlooking a portico. Contemporary sources say that in one of these "chambers", decorated for mourning, Ludovico il Moro took refuge in the throes of desperation due to the death of his wife Beatrice d'Este in 1497. Leonardo da Vinci painted the decorations in one of the rooms, but this work has not survived. The graffiti on the portico walls, reproducing ancient views of the Castle, were found during 20th-century restoration work.

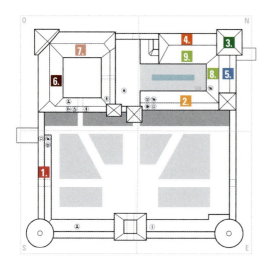

1. p. 32
The *Pietà Rondanini* Museum-Michelangelo

2. p. 38
The Museum of Ancient Art

3. p. 54
The Sala delle Asse

4. p. 58
The Museum of Furniture
and Wooden Sculptures

5. p. 66
The Picture Gallery

6. p. 76
The Museum of Decorative Arts

7. p. 84
The Museum of Musical Instruments

8. p. 92
The Museum of Archaeology
The Prehistory and Protohistory Section

9. p. 96
The Museum of Archaeology
The Egyptian Section

The Castle Museums

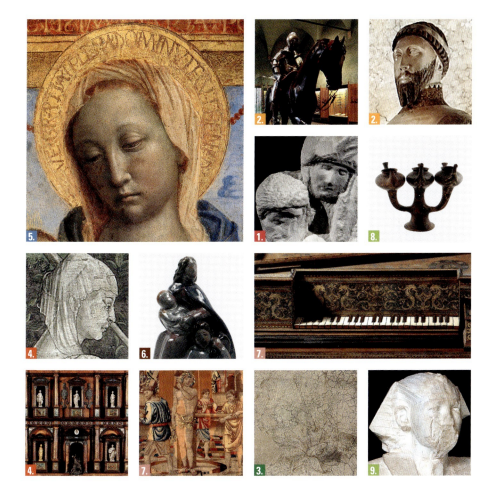

1. The *Pietà Rondanini* Museum-Michelangelo

On 2 May 2015 the Sforza Castle was enriched with a new museum dedicated to the last masterpiece made by Michelangelo Buonarroti (1475-1564). Situated in the former Spanish Hospital, in a space that originally hosted the sick and the plague-stricken, the museum can now be visited in the sober and evocative installation conceived by the architect Michele De Lucchi. As well as the *Pietà*, on display are a coin executed by Leone Leoni (ca. 1509-1590) of a portrait of Michelangelo, cast in the late 16th century, and a bronze portrait bust of the sculptor made by his pupil Daniele da Volterra (ca. 1509-1566), who used a wax death mask as a model.

The Building
In 1535 Milan fell under Spanish domination, and the Castle became the headquarters of the Iberian garrison. It was thus endowed with the modern fortifications and amenities needed by the soldiers living there. Sancho de Guevara y Padilla, castellan from 1574 to 1580 and governor of Milan from 1580 to 1583, had a hospital built for the troops. For this purpose a building adjoining the western walled curtain, decorated with paintings on the ceiling and walls, was remodelled. The date inscribed in Roman letters MD/LXXVII (1577) still visible today on the short side southwards probably refers to the end of the decorative work, coinciding with the outbreak in the city of the "plague of Saint Charles".

The hospital included a room with three painted square bays, each of which illuminated by a window overlooking the Cortile delle Armi, and by three side rooms made out of the walled curtain.

Towards the Castle's inner moat were areas used as an apothecary, a workshop, and a store, all of which were lost following Luca Beltrami's restoration work in 1907. The little information that has been discovered leads us to believe that the hospital was still functioning in the early 19th century.

opposite page
Monochrome red decoration on the facade of the Spanish Hospital, made by Luca Beltrami during restoration work (1907-1908), detail

right
The facade of the Spanish Hospital facing the Cortile delle Armi

The Painted Decoration

The ceiling is decorated with tondi framed by plant garlands that must have at one time contained the effigies of the twelve apostles, deduced by the names Peter, Andrew, and John in the first bay, on the side opposite the current entrance. Fancy scrolls containing inscriptions in capital letters that are still legible today feature the lines of the Apostle's creed. The taste and ornamental style show analogies with contemporary Lombard frescoes, close to Aurelio Luini and his workshop, active in Milan and Lombardy in the second half of the 16th century.

The illusionistic paintings on the walls, recognizable on both of the longer ones, divide the space by imitating wide pilasters, classical tympana on the windows, and fake trabeations.

The shorter walls of the room instead still feature the Spanish coats of arms. On the northern wall is the Coat of Arms of Spain, a grandiose shaped shield, with the chain of the Order of the Golden Fleece topped by the Spanish Royal crown. At the centre of the coat of arms is the insignia for the State of Milan. The fact that the insignia for Portugal, conquered in 1580, is missing offers a *terminus ante quem* for the execution of the painting.

On the opposite wall the insignia to the right and below features a shield divided into four parts, with the insignia of the family of the castellan and patron Sancho de Guevara y Padilla, that of the governor Antonio Guzman (1573-1580), and that of the Mendoza family. All that remains of the other insignia are traces, in the upper portion, of the helmet and ornaments that also belonged to the Padillas.

Restoration and Transformation Into the Museum

Between 1907 and 1908 the architect Luca Beltrami played his part in the hospital building, which he attributed to the early 16th century. Funded by the Mangili family, recalled in the commemorative plaque on the building's facade, Beltrami's work was limited to the demolition of the upper floor, built between the 18th and 19th centuries, and to the redecoration of the outer facade, with monochrome red motifs that Beltrami chose inspired by the vaults of the early 16th-century Milanese church of Santa Maria della Fontana. The plaques bearing the names of the artists and architects who worked on the Sforza Castle over the centuries are also due to Beltrami. Since July 2013, the decision to transform the historical building into the new museum for the *Pietà* has involved complex restoration work to reinforce the structure and endow it with the necessary anti-seismic and anti-vibration protection for Michelangelo's last masterpiece.

Michelangelo, the *Pietà Rondanini*

In the very last work he made, Michelangelo created a moving and intense deposition of the dead Christ held up by his Mother who is standing.

Based on the little information available it can be hypothesized that Michelangelo began to rough-hew the marble for the *Pietà Rondanini* between 1553 and 1555. In 1553, in fact, Ascanio Condivi made no mention of the *Pietà* in the artist's biography, while Giorgio Vasari, in 1555, did speak of a work since identified by scholars as the *Pietà Rondanini*.

In the final years of his life the artist worked on the sculptural group at different times, constantly changing his mind and modifying its composition. He changed the proportions of the body of Christ, making the bust and legs thinner, lowering and attenuating the head, which had at first been higher up and closer to that of his Mother; her face had originally turned right from the viewer's viewpoint, and diverged. Michelangelo also modified Christ's arms, which he leaned up against and merged into the his Mother's body.

Still visible from the first version of the *Pietà a*re Christ's right arm, broken to the elbow, which Michelangelo probably meant to eliminate later; the legs, which he had already begun to make thinner; the Mother's back, which the artist did not have a chance to reduce in order to rebalance the whole composition, before his death.

Two letters from Daniele da Volterra to Giorgio Vasari and to the master's nephew Leonardo Buonarroti, written in the months after Michelangelo's death, describe how the artist indefatigably chiselled the work, which he made for himself and considered to be his last will and testament, until just a few days before his death at the age of eighty-nine.

The *Pietà Rondanini* after Michelangelo

All trace of the sculptural group, mentioned in the inventory that Pope Pius IV had taken immediately after the artist's death (19 February 1564), was lost until 13 August 1807, when it was discovered to be the property of Giuseppe Rondinini (name later changed to Rondanini), a collector of paintings and more than two hundred sculptures, many of which distinguished, like the *Pietà,* by the initials M.G.R. Both palazzo and statue changed hands several times until, in 1946, the *Pietà* was transferred to a villa in Via Nerola. It was finally acquired in 1952 by the City of Milan, which placed it among the Castle's Civiche Raccolte d'Arte. The arrival of the *Pietà* from Rome on 1 November 1952 forced the architectural firm BBPR (Banfi, Belgiojoso, Peressutti and Rogers) engaged in the difficult task of designing the Castle museums to significantly alter their original plan. Taking up the challenge, the architects created an isolated space in the Sala degli Scarlioni, demolishing the ancient 15th-century vaults of the room located below it. The *Pietà,* surrounded by a pietra serena niche and accessed by walking down a staircase, was the last work that museum-goers would see when they visited the Museum of Ancient Art. It remained there until the spring of 2015.

2. The Museum of Ancient Art

Set within the solemn frame of the rooms overlooking the Corte Ducale, the Museum of Ancient Art, one of Italy's largest sculpture collections, houses about four hundred works, most of which come from the buildings and structures that were built inside Milan's medieval city walls. This unique patrimony includes sculptures originally located in city monasteries and the Duomo, votive statues decorating the city gates, the coats of arms and portals of the noble residences; stretching from the 5th to the 16th centuries, it documents the taste and style of prevalently Lombard artists, flanked by significant contributions by masters from Tuscany and beyond.

Along with this wealth of sculptures, the museum preserves commemorative stones and inscriptions dated to between the 5th and the 20th centuries of essential historical value, such as the *Stone of the Consuls* (dated to 1178) and the *Stone of Ausonius* (carved in the 16th century), a section containing about one hundred 19th-century plaster casts, and a vast repertory of decorative and terracotta tiles, including the *Busts of the Emperors* from the Milanese seat of the Medici Bank. The visit also offers a view of the sumptuous rooms with antique frescoes, the famous Sala delle Asse painted by Leonardo (Room VIII), and the Armory (Room XIV). The rooms hosting the Museo d'Arte Antica preserve traces, extensively restored in the late 19th century, of the splendid residence of Galeazzo Maria Sforza and of Ludovico il Moro. Three rooms instead document the age of Spanish domination. Rooms II, IV, and VII were in fact decorated on the occasion of the marriage in 1554 between the Infante of Spain and Duke of Milan Philip of Habsburg (future King Philip II) and his cousin Mary Tudor, Queen of England and Ireland.

The History

The museum is due to the passionate activity in the late-18th century by several scholars of Milan engaged in preventing the objects related to the city's art and history located in the demolished churches and monasteries from being dispersed. Their choices gave rise to the formation of collections that over the course of the 19th century entered the permanent museums.

Lombard sculptor, panel with symbols of the Evangelists, Musso-Olgiasca marble, early decades of the 12th century

One of the protagonists of this first phase was Giuseppe Bossi, secretary of Brera Academy, as well as being a collector and Leonardo scholar. In the second half of the 19th century two institutions of key importance to the birth of the museum were founded in Milan: the Museo Patrio di Archeologia, a state-owned foundation (1862), and the Museo Artistico Municipale, established by the civic administration (1878). When the Castle was restored and chosen to house the city's artistic mementoes, the holdings of the two museums were joined, and thus became the Museo Archeologico e Artistico, opened to the public on 10 May 1900. On 12 April 1956, after major restoration and work to install the holdings, the Museum of Ancient Art opened, a permanent exhibition of the sculptural works and architectural monuments that document Lombard art from the Early Middle Ages to the Renaissance.

The Exhibits
In the first exhibits dated to 1900, directed by Luca Beltrami with the assistance of Carlo Ermes Visconti and Giulio Carotti, the pre-Roman, Greek, Etruscan, and Roman antiquities were placed in the first rooms on the ground floor, while the successive rooms in the Sforza apartments, the Corte Ducale, and the Portico dell'Elefante housed the rich collection of medieval objects, with architectural elements such as capitals and corbels almost completely covering the walls.
Over the course of the first half of the 20th century the choice and display of the works gradually improved thanks to the efforts of Carlo Vicenzi and later Giorgio Nicodemi, scientific conservators of the collections. A significant turnaround took place after the Second World War with the new exhibit design by the architectural firm of Banfi, Belgiojoso, Peressutti, Rogers (BBPR), who began working in the Castle in the 1950s in collaboration with Costantino Baroni, director of collections. Designed on the basis of what was unanimously believed to be cutting-edge criteria, the Museum of Ancient Art offered a learned dialogue between the historical setting and the works exhibited.

2. Must-see
in the Museum of Ancient Art

a. Room II

Decorated in the age of Spanish domination, for the marriage between the future King of Spain Philip II and Mary Tudor in 1554, the ceiling features bouquets of flowers and fruit, boding well for the prosperity of the sovereigns. The lunettes contain the painted coats of arms of the patrons Don Fernando Alvarez of Toledo and Don Gomez Suarez of Figueroa, castellans of Milan in 1555 and in 1557, respectively.

b. Bonino da Campione and collaborators, *Mausoleum of Bernabò Visconti*, marble with traces of gilding and polychromy, 1360-1385/ca. 1386

The equestrian monument of Bernabò Visconti as a soldier, on horseback, in parade armour and wearing a helmet, was commissioned by the lord of Milan himself before 1363, and placed behind the altar of the Basilica of San Giovanni in Conca, adjoining the Visconti residence.

The sculptural group, which includes a base made up of columns and pillars and the imposing statue of Bernabò Visconti with the allegorical figures of *Justice* e *Fortitude* by his side, was carved from a single block of Candoglia marble and decorated with gold and silver painting. In 1385, after the sudden death of his uncle and father-in-law, Bernabo's nephew Gian Galeazzo Visconti used the equestrian monument as a tomb, adding a sarcophagus.

The short sides of the ark were also carved by Bonino *(Doctors of the Church and Coronation of the Virgin)*, while previously carved panels were used for the longer sides *(Christ as the Man of Sorrows between the Saints, The Crucifixion of Christ with the Saints and the Deceased)*. It is likely that these panels came from a tomb, perhaps that of a young Visconti, portrayed in the scene of the *Crucifixion*.

Bonino (1357-1393) created an evocative, balanced ensemble, achieving peaks of virtuosity in the rendering of the ornaments on Bernabò's armour, and the horse tack.

Visconti is immortalized holding the staff of command, dressed in armour embellished with his insignias and with the words in ancient French with the motto: "Suffering is my virtue but true suffering is to desist".

The sculpture, one of the masterpieces of Lombard statuary, has been in the Castle since 1898.

Room III

This room was at one time the chapel of San Donato. On the vault is a *Resurrection of Christ*, probably commissioned by Galeazzo Maria Sforza and executed before 1477.

c. Giovanni di Balduccio and assistants, *Tabernacle of Porta Ticinese*, marble, 1336-1338

A precious witness to the presence in Milan from about 1334 of a great artist like Giovanni di Balduccio da Pisa (known of from 1318 to 1349), the tabernacle is part of an important decorative campaign promoted by Azzone and Giovanni Visconti between 1336 and the mid-14th century. The lords of Milan had the doors of the medieval wall adorned with marble tabernacles which always represented the Virgin and Child, and Saint Ambrose, patron saint of Milan, in the act of demonstrating a model of the city quarter. The group was completed with three saints, titulars of churches in that area, or else the subject of particular veneration, for a sort of "sacred geography" of the city. The Pisan sculptor designed the whole series, executing by his own hand only some of the statues, however. Of these tabernacles, exhibited in the museum at the same level as their original location, those for the Ticinese, Orientale and Comasina gates have survived. The first of these, in which the central group is joined by Saints Lawrence, Eustorgius and Peter Martyr, reveals the hand of Giovanni di Balduccio in the expressive statues of the Virgin and Saint Peter Martyr. The sculptor used different stones for the latter figure to express the statue's polychromy.

Room IV

The coat of arms of Philip II King of Spain and his wife Mary Tudor dominate the room, surrounded by an assortment of decorations featuring flowers and fruit.

Room VII Sala del Gonfalone

The decorations in the room again refer to the royal marriage between Philip II King of Spain and Mary Tudor in 1554; the Royal Spanish coats of arms are surrounded by hawthorn shoots. Beneath the lunettes decorated with the coats of arms of the Spanish aristocratic families is a frieze with grotesques.

d. The Gonfalon of Milan, embroidery, tempera, and precious stones, 1565-1566

Commissioned by the Magnifica Comunità di Milano in 1565, the Gonfalon (standard) was

f.

completed in 1566. On 8 September, it was unveiled to the citizens and blessed by the Archbishop Carlo Borromeo. Executed using a sophisticated technique by Scipione Delfinone and Camillo da Posterla to a design by Giuseppe Arcimboldi and Giuseppe Meda, visible on both sides of the Gonfalon is St. Ambrose, patron saint of Milan.

Room VIII The Sala delle Asse
See section 3, pages 54-57.

e. Room XI Sala dei Ducali
On the ceiling are the four coats of arms of Galeazzo Maria Sforza against a blue background, with the painted initials "GZ MA" and the title "DVX MLI" (Galeazzo Maria Duke of Milan).

f. Agostino di Duccio, *Saint Sigismund on a Journey to Agaunum*, marble, 1449-1452
Executed by the Tuscan sculptor Agostino di Duccio (1418 – ca.1481) for the altar of the chapel of San Sigismondo in the Malatesta Temple in Rimini, the bas-relief was removed from the chapel in 1581.
Having ended up on the antiquarian market it was fortunately purchased by the Brera Academy Board in 1812.
The scene shows the journey of expiation of

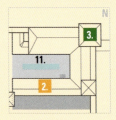

the Christian king of the Burgundians Saint Sigismund towards the city of Agaunum in Narbonese Gaul and the founding of the monastery.

In the artist's harmonious use of line, in the preciousness of the relief, in the allusion to the classical world, clearly visible in the angel that appears to show the way, echoing the scheme of a maenad, the sculptor reveals the high quality of his art, influenced by great Tuscan sculpture, from Ghiberti to Donatello. The bas-relief was carved between 1449 and 1452, the date the chapel of San Sigismondo was consecrated, the first in the Malatesta Temple to be completed.

g. *Room XII* **Ducal Chapel**

Galeazzo Maria Sforza had the chapel built in 1473 by Benedetto Ferrini and Bartolomeo Gadio and frescoed by a group of painters among whom Bonifacio Bembo, Giacomino Vismara and Stefano De Fedeli.

Sforza intended to build a chapel to welcome the twenty-two cantors chosen from the courts of all of Europe.

The background of the walls in gilded pastiglia features the rayed sun, an emblem the patron was particularly fond of, while the lunettes still show the faded images of the Sforza coats of arms. The vault motif of the guards at the sepulchre has an unusual iconography: instead of sleeping, at the time of the Resurrection, the soldiers seem to almost leap into the air and fall back down to the ground in awkward poses. Used as a barn during foreign occupation, the chapel, which lost one of its walls and whose frescoes were severely damaged, was restored in the early 20th century.

h. **Francesco Galli called Napoletano,** *Virgin and Child* (*Madonna Lia*), oil on canvas, ca. 1495

This stunning *Madonna Lia* painted by Francesco Napoletano gets its name from the collector Amedeo Lia, who generously donated it to the museum in 2007. Painted by a pupil of Leonardo, the tender couple formed by the Virgin and Child stands out against the bright landscape.

To the left is the Castle facade as it was in the Sforza era, before the explosion that destroyed the Filarete Tower in 1521.

i. *Room XIII* **Sala delle Colombine**
The emblem of the columbine in the radiant set against a red background and the motto "à bon droit" (rightly) repeated over and over as if to replicate a textile are a tribute to Galeazzo Maria Sforza and to his ancestors the Visconti.

I. Venetian sculptor, *Tabernacle with Figures of Angels,* **marble, second half of the 15th century**
At one time provided with a central door, which probably hid an enthroned Virgin, the tabernacle features two groups of angels within a space in Renaissance taste. The sculptor used the *stiacciato* technique (very flat, low relief) to make the subtle marble panels and create a composition of classical dimensions, in which the figures wearing roomy, light robes are described in a very fine relief.

Due to these characteristics, the unnamed author is included among the masters active in Venice in the second half of the 15th century. After belonging to the collection of Giuseppe Bossi, the precious tabernacle joined the Museo Patrio di Archeologia in 1864, together with the rest of the collection owned by the secretary of Brera Academy.

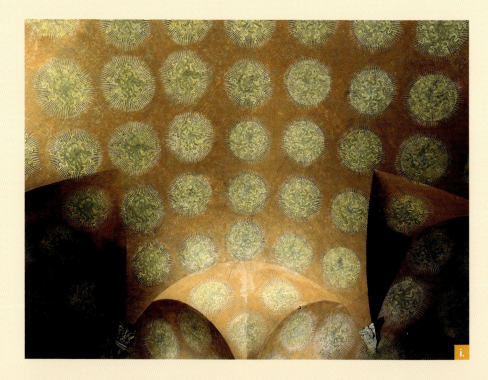

I.

MUST-SEE IN THE MUSEUM OF ANCIENT ART

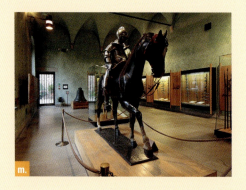

Room XIV The Armory

The Sala Verde, a brightly lit, spacious room on the ground floor of the Corte Ducale, hosts the Armory, devoted to cold weapons and firearms and their history from the late 14th to the 16th centuries. The first core of the museum was established in 1900, when the collection of weapons from the Museo Artistico Municipale and Brera Academy were installed in the Castle; in 1848 the Brera Academy, together with the collection of Uboldo weapons (later the property of the City) was looted by the citizens of Milan who needed weapons to fight with during the "Five Days of Milan". Over the years, the Armory has been added to by private donations, especially those of Count Bazzero de Mattei (1919) and Ambrogina Bergomi Subert (1941). During the 1943 air raids the collection was transferred to the warehouses and reinstalled in the Sala Verde in 1956, where it can still be seen today with a new arrangement. The weapons are displayed chronologically and by theme. It begins with the appearance, alongside traditional cold weapons, of the first hand-held bombards, and the evolution in the way war was waged on foot or on horseback, as well as in the forging of different weapon types. There are examples of armour (that of knights, gunmen, infantrymen, heavy and light cavalrymen), in which corsets to protect the body, and groups of weapons of the same kind, stand out: cold arms, like javelins, swords, infantrymen and cavalrymen headdress, and firearms, from arquebuses to revolvers, with ever-improved firing devices. Some finely made Milanese pieces from the 15th, 16th, and 17th centuries include a Venetian parade helmet, an umbo for a pump wheel, and a decorated corset, the work of the anonymous Master of the Castle. Among the heirlooms is the sabre of Marshal Radetzky (1766-1858). Also on view are materials, especially from the Renaissance, related to the military world and to the artistic and historical events of Milan, for centuries the seat of illustrious gunsmithing workshops. These are the portals of an important Milanese palazzo no longer in existence, including the Medici Bank, works from the city's churches, such as the reliefs by the sculptor Giovanni Antonio Amadeo (1447-1522), the gravestones of noblemen and men of arms, Sforza coats of arms and emblems in stone, the 1601 celebratory monument of the Count of Fuentes, governor of Milan. Heraldry and arms also appear in the 17th-century multicoloured glasswork that is part of the large windows.

n.

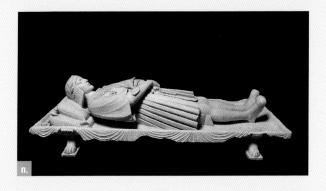
n.

Room XV Sala degli Scarlioni

For the room that was used for closed hearings and the secret council, the Sforza chose the typical zigzag pattern they referred to as "scarlioni", currently visible after the extensive restoration work carried out in the late 19th century.

n. Agostino Busti, called Il Bambaia, *Funerary Monument of Gaston de Foix*, marble, 1517-1522

The funerary monument commissioned by Francis I King of France in honour of the hero of Ravenna Gaston de Foix, who died on 11 April 1512 during his victorious campaign in Italy, was originally located in Santa Marta in Milan. The body of the very young lieutenant to Louis XII, was taken to this church, favoured by the French and the Milanese aristocracy, after the solemn funeral rites held in Milan Cathedral.

A document from 1517 refers to an "archa superba", but the end of French domination interrupted the works, and the elements were dispersed in private and public collections. The acquisition of the marble works in the Arconati collection (1990) brought most of the monument back to the museum.

In addition to the statue of Gaston, reliefs with the deeds of the hero, apostles, and allegorical figures have also been preserved. The classical composure of the lying figure is one of the high points in early 16th-century Milanese sculpture, and documents the finest season of Il Bambaia (1483-1548), master of a language that harmoniously merges echoes of classical culture, Michelangelo's inventions, and Leonardo's ability to reveal the depth of the soul in every figure. The marble surfaces are rendered with virtuoso skill, subtle and vibrant, and striated by light grooves.

3. The Sala delle Asse

Visiting the Museum of Ancient Art one enters Room VIII, the famous Sala delle Asse, painted by Leonardo da Vinci (1452-1519).

The "Chamber of the Dark Berries"
Referred to in the Sforza documents as the "Sala delle Asse" (referring to the wooden planks used to clad the Castle's humid rooms), the room on the ground floor of the Castellana Tower was given the name it is known by today by the architect Luca Beltrami in the late 19th century, based on these records. The decoration dates from 1498: the only sources that mention it are two letters dated 21 and 23 April of that same year, sent to Ludovico il Moro by the ducal chancellor Gualtiero Bescapè, which include the name of "magistro Leonardo" as concerns unspecified works in the room. For this work the Tuscan artist created an illusionistic pergola of mulberry trees imitating an open area inside the Castle. Records from that period, including the one by the famous mathematician Luca Pacioli (*De divina proportione*, 1509), recall the room as the "chamber of the *moroni*" – an explicit allusion to the mulberry.

A Pergola in a Room
Leonardo painted an intricate composition formed by the interweaving of fronds and sixteen mulberry trees adorned with strong gilded ropes. The choice of the solid and robust mulberry tree alluded to the soubriquet of Ludovico Sforza, called "il Moro" owing to his dark complexion, and it also recalled his role in the dissemination of the mulberry plantation responsible for the flourishing production of silk in Lombardy. Furthermore, from a symbolic point of view, using this particular plant, called *sapientissima omnium arborum*, was a way of celebrating Ludovico il Moro's political know-how, and the Duchy's stability under his rule. The plaques painted on the vault also recall the duke's successes, the alliance with Emperor Maximilian obtained through clever matrimonial politics, the awarding of the title of duke in 1495, and the victory at Fornovo against the French in 1496. The fourth plaque that had been planned for the vault was probably modified after the Moro's escape in 1499 with an inscription that recalled the taking of Milan by King Louis XII.

The Room during Foreign Domination
A sumptuous frame for the ceremony on 25 June 1511 when the French governor of Milan Francis II of Orleans passed on the power to the young Gaston de Foix, Duke of Nemours – as told by Alberto Vignati in *Memorie istoriche* written in 1519 –, the room ended up being used as a stable, like other rooms in the ducal apartments in the centuries that followed.

The Rediscovery of Leonardo and the Restoration Work of Luca Beltrami
When the Castle was taken over by the City of Milan on 25 October 1893, the ancient fortilice became the subject of research. Between 1893 and 1894, the German historian and Leonardo scholar Paul Müller-Walde identified fragments of the original decoration on the vault. A few years later, thanks to the generosity of Pietro Volpi, a lawyer, the restoration of the decoration was begun. Luca Beltrami hired the painter Ernesto Rusca who used fragments and clues to reconstruct the decorative motif of one ceiling section, entirely repainting it with thick bright tempera. At the inauguration that took place on 10 May 1902 there was talk of the rediscovery of the "real Leonardo", but some critical voices were raised against this much-debated restoration project. A few years later, the room was clad in reddish-purple tapestry and wooden benches were placed along the wall, hiding the Leonardesque monochrome, believed to be from the subsequent era.

The Restoration
As part of the redesigning of the Castle museums, the room was restored in 1955 by Ottemi Della Rotta, who chose to lighten up the intense colours that Rusca had used to create the effect of antique and abraded painting. After the diagnostic campaign that was started in 2006, in October 2013 the work by the Opificio delle Pietre Dure in Florence began. The restoration of the decoration had three aims: to arrest the cause of the painting's deterioration, to clean the surface, and to recuperate, where possible, the legibility of the original decoration. The work since carried out has led to some astonishing discoveries, such as portions of charcoal drawing on all the walls in the room, which had remained hidden under the plaster for over five centuries.

4. The Museum of Furniture and Wooden Sculptures

The museum, located on the first floor of the Corte Ducale, holds six centuries of the history of furniture; it is a high point in all of Italy and in particular Lombardy. The almost two thousand pieces are displayed by chronology and theme, showing how style and taste have changed, and how society evolved from the 15th to the 20th centuries. Providing a rich backdrop to the furniture are sculptures, objects, and tapestries. The 15th century is represented by the multifunctional *cassone*, often carved or painted, such as the *Chest of the Three Dukes* (Galeazzo Maria Sforza, Gian Galeazzo Maria and Ludovico il Moro); this piece, along with several rare objects among which the *Chalice of Ludovico il Moro*, evokes the splendour of the Corte Ducale at the Castle. But the oldest period is also documented by furniture and wooden sculptures that were used as religious furnishings. Of particular interest in the section devoted to the 16th-17th centuries is the *stipo*, which stored precious objects in drawers hidden by architectural perspectives, inlaid work, paintings, and carved figurines. This piece of furniture typically belonged to collectors, and was used to furnish *studioli* and "encyclopaedic" cabinets of curiosity. The 17th century was also the time of the eccentric, scenographic Baroque piece, i.e. chests, *consolles*, mirrors, chairs, and divans, furniture that reappeared in the 18th century in the more elegant Rococo style, rather widespread in Milan. Lastly, to illustrate the history of "designer" furniture – from the Rococo to the postmodern style of the 20th century – the exhibition continues with pieces made by the great masters: Maggiolini, Pogliaghi, Bugatti, Eugenio and Mario Quarti, Gio Ponti, Sottsass, Mendini. These were the leading names of Neoclassicism, of a revival of past styles (especially of the Renaissance), of Liberty, Déco, and 20th-century trends, at a time when there was lively debate about the relationship between art design and industrial furniture production. The exhibit has been arranged so that visitors can begin with contemporary furniture and work backwards.

The History

The Museum was formed thanks to gifts, bequests, the acquisition of objects that once belonged to the manufacturers' families, such as the cabinetmakers Mora, or to the members of Milan's aristocracy and haute bourgeoisie, such as the Sormani, Durini, Andreani, Boschi, as well as to loans from the residences of the Savoy in Milan and in Monza. Conceived by the BBPR firm in 1956 and extensively renovated in 1981, the current installation is the work of the architects Perry King and Santiago Miranda.

4. Must-see

in the Museum of Furniture and Wooden Sculptures

Room XVIII

a. **Milanese workshop**, Passalacqua Cabinet, wood, ivory, gilded bronze, silver, rock crystal, precious stones, oil painting on copper, 1613

Described by the canon of Como Cathedral Quintino Lucini Passalacqua, who commissioned the work, as a "very artificious writing-desk", the object comprises a lower part with cupboards, decorated with telamons in classical style, and an upper part with a drop-down lid, turning the cabinet into a writing-desk and unveiling its precious contents: a sumptuous palace with a facade filled with columns and niches, behind which are five ingeniously hidden drawers.

The ivory statues, made by Guillame Berthelot, symbolize the five senses; the copper sheets below them were oil painted by Morazzone with biblical scenes; the small bronze at the centre represents Reason dragged away by five wild animals that also embody the five senses. The whole decorative system, made according to the patron's indications and ideas about morality, encourage us to prevent the senses from overcoming reason.

Room XVI

b. **Giuseppe Maggiolini**, Chinoiserie-Decorated Chest, wood, gilded bronze, marble top, ca. 1773

A warm, enveloping light allows visitors to fully admire the refined elegance of the objects created by the Lombard cabinetmaker Giuseppe Maggiolini (1738-1814), represented in the museum by furniture of different styles and decorations, from the earliest works in Rococo taste, to the late ones in Empire Style. An ingenious interpreter of the artistic trends of his day and age, Maggiolini was affirmed by crafting in his successful workshop pieces that were perfect down to the minutest detail, made for demanding local and European patrons.

The master used dozens of different types of wood to create outstanding chromatic effects and embellished his furniture with decorations that were often designed by some of the finest artists. Since 1895 the Sforza Castle has owned one of the famed cabinetmaker's first pieces, a chest dated to around 1773: the rounded forms and bronze ornaments featuring theatre masks and Chinese figures hark back to Rococo tradition, echoed in the central medallions designed by Andrea Appiani. The inlay pattern is instead innovative.

Room XVI

c. **Ettore Sottsass,** *Casablanca* **Sideboard, decorated plastic laminate, 1981, Memphis edition 2003**

The objects made by Ettore Sottsass (1917-2007) bring the visitor face to face with a break with tradition. His pieces of furniture are the voice of a trend in Italian design that radically offsets "rationally" functional objects produced in a series, and devoid of originality. Sottsass, together with the Italian design and architecture group called Memphis (1981-1987), created exclusive objects with forms and colour choices that had an emotional and sensory effect.

The *Casablanca* sideboard, in fact, is more like a dynamic sculpture than a piece of furniture. Contrariwise, the materials used, i.e. plastic laminates, moulded glass, and veneer, albeit ennobled, belong to industrial production.

Room XVII
The Stories of Griselda
see pages 64-65

b.

MUST-SEE IN THE MUSEUM OF FURNITURE AND WOODEN SCULPTURES

4. The Stories of Griselda

Room XVII of the Museum of Furniture and Wooden Sculptures features the cycle of the *Stories of Griselda*, painted on the walls and ceiling.
The decorative cycle was detached, in 1897-1898, from a room in the south-western tower of Roccabianca Castle (Parma), and then reconstructed, respecting the original arrangement, in the Castle Pinacoteca (Picture Gallery), designed in the postwar period by the architectural firm BBPR (Banfi, Belgiojoso, Peressutti, Rogers).
Commissioned by Pier Maria Rossi, Count of Berceto, in the second half of the 15th century, the cycle features on the vault at the centre the *Sol Iustitiae* in stucco relief, surrounded by twenty bays representing the constellations, planets, and signs of the zodiac, in a rare iconography.
Narrated on the walls on two registers are the events in the life of Griselda, taken from the last story in the *Decameron* by Boccaccio (written between 1349 and 1353). The painter describes in images the tests that Gualtieri, Marquis of Saluzzo, forces his humble wife Griselda to undergo in order to measure her loyalty and obedience. Thanks to her outstanding patience, Griselda manages to pass every test and keep the family together.
This complex composition, made in monochrome grey on a green background with rare colour inserts, is attributed to a Lombard artist close to the style of Benedetto Bembo (known of from 1462 to 1493), a master from Cremona and the member of a family of painters active for both the Visconti and Sforza families.

5. The Picture Gallery

Located on the first floor of the Corte Ducale, the Picture Gallery, formed over time by the art collections of the aristocratic families and the collecting activity of illustrious citizens, patriots, and enthusiasts, traces the history of Milanese and Lombard art from the 15th to the 18th centuries, added to which are Venetian works and 17th-century Dutch-Flemish paintings. The many paintings on canvas and board by Lombard artists are accompanied by the works of some exceptional figures: Andrea Mantegna, Giovanni Bellini, Bronzino, Lorenzo Lotto, Correggio, Tintoretto and Canaletto.
In chronological order, altarpieces, paintings on board and canvas, frescoes, exhibited alongside sculptures, reliefs, medals and terracotta busts allow for comparisons to be made and reveal an interweaving of taste and style.
Also part of the Gallery's holdings are cycles of wall paintings and frescoes, including the one commissioned by Bernabò Visconti in San Giovanni in Conca in the mid-14th century, on display in the Museum of Ancient Art, or the famed *Griselda's Room,* painted in the 15th century, originally in the Roccabianca Castle in Parma, and reconstructed in the Museum of Furniture and Wooden Sculptures.

The History
Underlying the origins of the Picture Gallery are private art collections donated to the City to endow Milan with its own artistic heritage. The Fogliani Marchesi bequest of 1861, the Innocenzo and Gian Giacomo Attendolo Bolognini bequest of 1863, and the Antonio Guasconi bequest of 1863-1865, comprised the first generous donations of artworks to the city, and these were followed, for the entire second half of the 19th century, by other precious gifts, legacies, and loans.
On 2 June 1878 the Museo Artistico Municipale was opened in the hall of the Public Gardens, relocated to the Sforza Castle a few years later. In 1900, in this newly restored location, the Picture Gallery's oldest group of works was inaugurated. Located on the piano nobile, in what is now Room XXVI, the collection featured walls covered in detached frescoes and large-scale paintings, while the smaller-scale canvases and the works on board were placed on easels and

book stands, evocatively amassing the works so that the space resembled a storage area more than a museum. In the following years changes and improvements were made.
Over the course of the 20th century the Picture Gallery has enriched its holdings thanks to generous gifts and bequests but also to the acquisition by the City of items of particular interest, among which the Trivulzio Collection in 1935, which brought the paintings of Filippo Lippi and Mantegna to the Castle.
In 1995 two major works by Canaletto entered the collection, while in 2007 the generous gift of the collector Amedeo Lia enriched the Gallery with a painting by Francesco Napoletano, portraying the Castle itself as it was in the early 16th century, in the background of a sacred object.

The Exhibits
After it was solemnly inaugurated on 10 May 1900, the collection of antique paintings underwent several layouts, which can be reconstructed thanks to the photographs housed in the Castle Photographic Archive.
The growth in the number of works, the availability of display space, and the needs related to conservation and safety have determined the gradual transformation of the Picture Gallery; in the post-war period a first installation was designed by the BBPR firm in collaboration with Costantino Baroni, head of collections. In that layout, inaugurated in 1956, the paintings were hung on brickwork stage wings, each of which in a specific space and with the most suitable lighting. In the following arrangement, instead, curated in 1980 by the Albini-Helg-Piva firm, lightweight metal and fibreglass mesh served as a support for the works which appeared to be suspended in space. After the work that was done in 2005, the Picture Gallery took on its current appearance, designed by the architect Valter Palmieri and curated by Mauro Natale and Laura Basso. The works are exhibited from room to room, accentuating the discontinuous nature of the collection formed by coherent groups by individual authors and by authentic single paintings, allowing visitors to view the paintings, terracottas, medals, and sculptures, but also the Castle that hosts them all.

5. Must-see

in the Picture Gallery

Room XXI
a. Vincenzo Foppa, *Virgin and Child* (also called *Madonna of the Book*), tempera on board, ca. 1475

In this small-format painting, to be used for private devotion and that has become an icon of the Gallery, the great painter from Brescia Vincenzo Foppa (ca. 1430-1516), who endowed Milan with highly valued paintings and frescoes, seems to have been inspired by a sculptural model in the style of Donatello. The artist focuses on Mary's golden nimbus and small book, overlapping the frame from which the sacred characters look out.

Running along three sides of the frame, according to a solution used in Flemish painting, is an inscription praising the Virgin: "AVE SANCTIS[S]IMA MARIA PORTA PARADISI DOMINA MUNDI PURA SINGULARIS TU ES VIRGO SINGULARIS TU CONCEPISTI IESUM". This is the *incipit* of an oration attested to in the years of Sixtus IV's papacy (1471-1484) honouring the Immaculate Conception, a dogma that was being debated at the time by the Franciscans and the Dominicans. Inscribed in Mary's nimbus instead are the first words of the *Hail Mary*: "AVE GRATIA PLENA DOMINUS TECUM TU BENEDI[CTA]".

The skilful use of chiaroscuro with hazy shadows on the faces reveals the painter's knowledge of models from Flemish art, while the shiny string of dark red coral in the background and the heavy, almost embossed folds, are proof of Foppa's closeness to the Ferrarese school of painting.

Room XXIII
b. Giovanni Bellini, *Virgin and Child*, tempera on board, 1460-1465

In this small panel bearing the fragmentary signature of Giovanni Bellini (1432-1516), which can feasibly be considered authentic, the mother and child do not look at each other, although their hands are touching.

She tries to take the fruit away, an allusion to sin and thus the Passion that her Son will have to undergo to save humanity, while the Child tries to push his mother's arm away, looking closely at the piece of fruit.

The young Venetian artist and pre-eminent Renaissance painter already revealed his great skill in the way he made the child's green tunic, decorated with a golden border, and created the soft folds in Mary's rose-coloured cloak.

a.

Room XXIII

c. **Andrea Mantegna,** *Virgin in Glory and Saint John the Baptist, Gregory the Great, Benedict and Jerome,* **tempera on canvas, 1497**

Housed in the Gallery is a painting by Andrea Mantegna (1431-1506), a leading figure in Renaissance figurative culture. Court painter for the Gonzagas, Mantegna painted the *Bridal Chamber* in Mantua, a cycle executed in 1474, which made a lasting impression on Galeazzo Maria Sforza, as attested to in the documents. This altarpiece, which was painted to adorn the high altar of the church of Santa Maria in Organo in Verona, bears the painter's signature and the date, 15 August 1497, which refers to the Feast of the Assumption, protective of the church, on the scroll held by one of the singing angels: "A. MANTINIA PI/A[N] GRACIE/1497 15 AUGUST" (Andrea Mantegna painted in the year of grace

MUST-SEE IN THE PICTURE GALLERY

1497, 15 August). This intriguing work came to the Castle thanks to the City's acquisition of the Trivulzio Collection (1935). The Paduan master created a monumental composition in which the Virgin is not enthroned as per convention, but seems to be suspended in a luminous mandorla surrounded by cherubim, iconography alluding to Mary's ascent Heavenward. The four saints, John the Baptist, Gregory the Great, Benedict and Jerome, are seen from a lower perspective, rendering them solemn and monumental. The three angels in the lower part of the panel are portrayed before an organ, corresponding to the emblem of the Verona church. The scene is framed by two luxuriant trees laden with fruit.

Room XXVI
d. Giovanni Antonio Canal, known as Canaletto, *The Dock towards the Riva degli Schiavoni with the Column of Saint Mark*, oil on canvas, before 1742

This canvas and its pendant, *The Dock towards the Zecca with the Column of Saint Theodore*, are among the Gallery's masterpieces, joining the collection in 1995. A famed Venetian artist, Canaletto (1697-1768) achieves perfect balance in these works, bestowing clarity and emphasis on all the elements in the view, from the monumental architectures to the minuscule figures inhabiting this city on a lagoon, from the variations in the sky to the sparkling waters. Venice, illuminated by a clear and transparent light, appears to be portrayed in a moment of everyday life. If we look closely at the canvases, we glimpse before the monumental buildings and houses, and on the boats, the multitude of everyday figures going about their daily activities.

The notes of colour in the clothing and hats merge with the clear blue sky dotted with clouds, and with the green of the slightly rippling waters of the lagoon. The elegant carved and gilded wooden frames were made when the two canvases were commissioned, prior to 1742.

e. Bernardo Bellotto, *The Palace of the Giureconsulti and the Milan Broletto*, oil on canvas, 1744

Nephew on his mother's side of Canaletto, with whom he trained from 1735, Bernardo Bellotto (ca. 1721-1780) devoted himself from the 1740s to *vedutista* painting distinguished by intense realism and deliberate attention to the objective elements of reality examined from every angle, including the humblest and most modest ones.

This canvas on a Milanese subject, part of a significant group of views of the Lombard *contado* painted around 1744, was present from 1750 in an English collection. It did not return to Milan until 1998.

The unusual vertical slant of the work offers a view of one of the city's streets before the additions made in the late 18th century and the major urban transformation that followed.

On a bright day, squeezed between the Broletto and the palazzo dei Giureconsulti, Via Mercanti is brought to life with the activities of the many figures depicted.

Bellotto painted the view rather close up, describing with minutious care the rough stone facade of the medieval Broletto and the refined marble of the palazzo dei Giureconsulti built later, from which the Napo Torriani house-tower rises high.

d.

6. The Museum of Decorative Arts

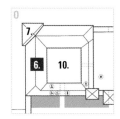

Italy's most important collection of decorative arts is displayed in some of the rooms of the Corte Ducale and on the first and second floors of the Rocchetta. Over the course of the 20th century the museum received precious gifts from private citizens and benefited from the fervent acquisitions activity of the Castle directors. The works belong to different material types: tapestries, arms, ivories, bronzes, ceramics (sgraffito ware, majolica, porcelain), leather, wrought iron, furniture, gold and enamelled objects, clocks, wooden sculptures, scientific instruments, textiles, lacework, glassware. The exhibition route currently undergoing renewal is filled with masterpieces and objects of excellent quality that document the evolution in taste and style in the applied arts from Early Christianity until the 20th century in Italy and Europe. Among the most significant collections to have entered the museum is the Mora Collection, 1908, with about six hundred wooden objects and various textiles, the Trivulzio Collection, 1935, including famous tapestries, along with examples of fine goldsmithing, ivory, incunabula, paintings, and sculptures, and Late Antiquity ivories collected and donated by the painter Giuseppe Bossi, secretary of Brera Academy and himself a collector. Along with the antique works there are numerous contemporary decorative art objects of great artistic value, acquired between 1923 and 1941 from the International Exhibitions of Decorative Art. The collection is completed by Gianguido Sambonet's collection of two thousand pieces of cutlery, the only one of its kind chronologically speaking, as it stretches from the Egyptian age to our day, and quality-wise. Acquired by the Lombardy Region in 1997, the collection is on a twenty-year loan to the Museum of Decorative Arts.

The History
The Museo Artistico Municipale first opened its doors on 2 June 1878, merging the remarkable collection of objects owned by the City, that had joined the collection over the course of the 19th century via gifts and bequests, with the holdings of the Museum of Industrial Arts. From its initial location in the hall of the Public Gardens in Corso Venezia, the museum was relocated to the Castle and was opened on 10 May 1900. After the damage that was done to the Castle during both World Wars, a contract for the remodelling of the museum was awarded to the BBPR architecture firm. Around the year 2000 the museum in the Castle was again renovated.

6. Must-see

in the Museum of Decorative Arts

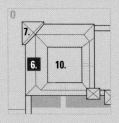

a. *The Marys at the Tomb*, ivory, early 5th century

This refined ivory tablet, the only valve of a diptych to have been preserved, and part of the Trivulzio Collection, is one of the rare objects to have joined the museum illustrated with a religious subject.

The scene, one of the oldest known representations of the Holy Sepulchre, is divided into two registers. Represented above, under the two Evangelists, Luke symbolized by the bull and Matthew by the angel, is the Holy Sepulchre. In the lower register the two women meet a figure, the angel or perhaps Jesus Christ risen.

In the background the shutters of the door feature three Gospel scenes, the *Resurrection of Lazarus*, *Zacchaeus Climbs Up a Tree to See Jesus*, and *Christ Taming the Crowd*.

Based on style the tablet is dated to the early 5th century.

b. Lombard workshop, *Voghera Monstrance*, partially gilded and enamelled silver, 1456

This remarkable piece was acquired in 1915 from the Collegiata di San Lorenzo in Voghera (Pavia) thanks to a gift to the Raccolte Civiche by the Countess Luisa Morelli di Popolo in memory of her husband Galeazzo Visconti. The architectural complexity, the vibrant colours, and the large size make this monstrance one of the museum's most important examples of 15th-century silversmithing.

The inscription niellated in the stem bears the name of the Collegiata di San Lorenzo for which it was created, and the date 26 May 1456: "Completum fuit hoc tabernaculum pro plebe viqueriensi diocesis tortoniensis MCCCCLVI die XXVI madii".

previous page
Arturo Martini, *The Flight into Egypt*, majolica, 1927

b.

c. **Urbino, Patanazzi workshop, Ewer, majolica, ca. 1585**

This precious majolica ewer, together with an amphora, a platter, and a goblet exhibited in the museum, were part of the dinner service featuring the motto "ARDET IN AETERNUM" (burning forever), commissioned by the Duke of Ferrara Alfonso II d'Este for his marriage to Margherita Gonzaga in 1579.

The Patanazzi workshop, renowned makers of earthenware active in Urbino in the second half of the 16th century, was hired to make this object. The emblem painted on the neck of the ewer represents the asbestos stone in flames. This mineral, whose Greek name means inextinguishable, and the motto "burning forever", framed in two curved scrolls between two sphinxes, symbolically exalt the flame of love and the fact that it cannot be extinguished. The upper and lower parts are decorated in

a.

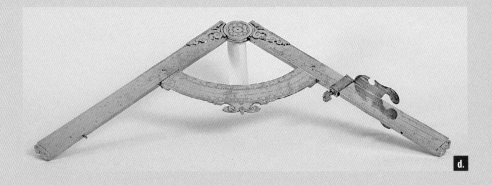

"grotesques" with birds and fantastic creatures, while painted on the middle part are marine deities, among which a river god holding an oar between two half-centaur, half-triton figures; these motifs were inspired by the painting of Raphael, whose subjects were borrowed from and spread through prints.

d. Geometric military compass designed by Galileo Galilei, gilded copper, Padua, 1606

Conceived by Galileo Galilei in 1597 to facilitate the execution of complex calculations, a mere five copies of the geometric compass entered the collection, one of which is exhibited in the Museum of Decorative Arts.

This instrument, besides allowing for the quick execution of at least forty types of geometric and arithmetic operations based on the mechanism of proportions, could be used to solve problems of a civil and especially military nature.

The compass could determine the proper charge for a cannon, it could redesign a map in different scales, and it could compute money exchange rates. Galileo described how it worked in the treatise *Operations of the Geometric and Military Compass*; published in 1606 Padua in sixty copies, the treatise was sold or given out with the sector itself.

e. Gio Ponti and Libero Andreotti for Richard Ginori, *Blue Lidded Box*, porcelain, 1928

Produced by the Richard Ginori Manufactory, this precious piece of porcelain was conceived by the versatile architect and designer Gio Ponti (1891-1979), an eminent figure in the renewal of 20th-century Italian decorative arts. Ponti managed to reconcile production in a series and the individuality of craftsmanship, conceiving groups of objects with the same shape but in different colours, or using the same design to decorate very different objects. Celebrated on this elegant lidded box set against a blue background are Love and Death standing on chariots drawn by winged horses, alternated with allegorical triumphal arches. This cylindrical vase sits on gilded feet topped by resting angels that, along with the handle on the lid, were made to a design by the famous Tuscan sculptor Libero Andreotti (1875-1933).

e.

7. The Museum of Musical Instruments

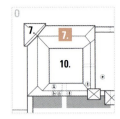

The Castle owns one of the most important collections of musical instruments in Italy and Europe, about nine hundred pieces ranging from the 16th to the 20th centuries. Exhibited on the first and second floor of the Rocchetta, they can be viewed in all their variety, complexity, and fine decoration. The first two rooms of the museum are devoted to the collection of the Monzino, a Milanese family of makers and sellers of instruments active from the mid-18th to the 20th centuries. The tools and materials used by luthiers, and parts of instruments as they are crafted allow visitors to get some idea of the skill and passion required to do this type of work. These are followed by instruments from the 17th-19th centuries representing the great luthiers of the Monzino house: the instruments are traditional and yet unique, such as the archguitar, the harp guitar, and the mandolyre. The instruments that follow are organized into groups, the first of which dedicated to ethnic music, the following ones to Italian and European tradition, represented by schools, workshops, and famous craftsmen. On display are: violins, violas, violoncellos, bass viols and violas da gamba; lutes, guitars, mandolas and mandolins; flutes, clarinets, oboes and bassoons; clavichords, harpsichords, spinettes, virginals, organs, forte-pianos and pianofortes. Also included in the collection are harps, hurdy-gurdies, psalteries and several brasses, as well as some little-known instruments like the pochette and the glass harmonica. Lastly, on view is the equipment of the Rai Studio di Fonologia Musicale di Milano, which produced electronic experimental music between 1955 and 1983, and realized sound comments for radio and television. The museum plays an active part in the field of dissemination and music: some of the instruments are still used so that audiences can have the privilege of listening to antique sounds in magical locations.

The History

The museum was opened in Palazzo Morando in 1958, after the City of Milan acquired the valuable collection owned by maestro Natale Gallini (1891-1983). In 1963 the museum was transferred to the Castle, specifically to the Rocchetta, in a space designed by the BBPR architecture firm still partly preserved today. New materials were added to the Gallino Collection through gifts and acquisitions. These included the bequest of the engineer and violinist Antonio Boschi and the gift of the Monzino Collection by the Fondazione "De Musica" in 2000. In 2008 a dedicated space was designed by the De Lucchi firm to house the Rai Studio di Fonologia Musicale di Milano with original decor by Gio Ponti.

7. Must-see

in the Museum of Musical Instruments

Room XXXVI

a. **Giovanni Grancino**, Viola, maple, fir, poplar, walnut, ebony, ivory, mother-of-pearl, tortoise shell, gold leaf, Milan, 1662, Natale Gallini Collection

One of the main groups in the Castle's collection is made up of string instruments, particularly violins and violas, which belong to the same family.

Originating in the 16th century and still being played as a solo and orchestra instrument, the viola has undergone the same evolution as the Baroque string instruments, modified and modernized from the 18th century to satisfy new musical needs. Except for the paint, this viola made by Giovanni Grancino (1637-1709), a member of an illustrious family of luthiers from Milan, has remained remarkably unaltered.

This instrument, still played today, is distinguished for its unusual lobed profile, and the elegant inlaid decoration on the fingerboard and tailpiece, in which ebony, mother-of-pearl, and tortoise shell alternate, mounted on gold leaf to accentuate the reflections.

b. **Giovanni Maria Anciuti**, Oboe, ivory and gilded silver, Milan, 1722, Venerosi Pesciolini Collection

The oboe, which the museum has several copies of, is one of the most important wood instruments in the classical orchestra, giving the "concert pitch" at the start of performances; thanks to its expressive qualities, it is often used for solos. Although invented in Antiquity, it was in 17th-century France when Louis XIV was in rule that the oboe evolved into its current form; it was later innovated in the 20th century.

Visitors can also see an exceptional instrument acquired in 1997, an ivory oboe made in 1722 by Giovanni Maria Anciuti (1674-1744); only the finest workmanship was used to make it, and it is aesthetically very beautiful, still perfect and technically innovative. Thanks to the ingeniousness of its maker it is endowed with a spare upper section, making it possible to vary intonation, a solution that would spread from the mid-18th century onwards.

MUST-SEE IN THE MUSEUM OF MUSICAL INSTRUMENTS

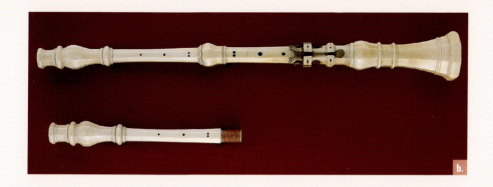

Room XXXVII **Sala della Balla**
c. **Ioannes Ruckers**, **Double Virginal**, poplar, fir, oak, beech, printed paper, Antwerp, ca. 1600, Natale Gallini Collection

The virginal, like the harpsichord and the spinette, is one of the keyboards instruments in which the chords are plucked while playing. Widespread and appreciated from the 16th to the 18th centuries, it is well represented in the Castle collection; this type of instrument was gradually replaced by the pianoforte, the protagonist of 19th-century music. The Low Countries were among the main producers in Europe, especially Antwerp, home to one of the most famous families of harpsichord makers, the Ruckers; Ioannes Ruckers is the author of the double virginal at the Castle. This instrument belongs to the type called "mother-son", in which a larger virginal (mother) is flanked, to the right, by a smaller removable one (son). The two keyboards could thus be played at the same time by two musicians, or, when placed one atop the other, by one musician.

This instrument is also of interest owing to the elegance of the zoomorphic and plant decorations covering the surface, printed on paper and painted in tempera, and to the painting that graces the interior of the lid. Ladies and gentlemen are depicted as they enjoy themselves hunting, sailing, conversing, reading, and playing: unsurprisingly, one lady is portrayed under a *berceau* as she plays a virginal, it too decorated by a musical scene.

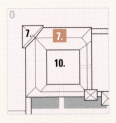

Room XXXVII **Sala della Balla**
d. e. **Bramantino,** *Trivulzio Tapestries*
This precious cycle of tapestries portraying the twelve months of the year exhibited in the Sala della Balla was commissioned by Gian Giacomo Trivulzio, appointed *maréchal* and governor-general of Lombardy by France in 1499. The tapestries, designed by Bartolomeo Suardi called Bramantino (known of from 1480 to 1530) and woven in Vigevano by Benedetto da Milano and collaborators, were finished in 1509.
The Trivulzio tapestries are exceptionally complete and in a good state of conservation; at the centre of each one is the month to which the tapestry is dedicated, surrounded by figures and instruments alluding to the corresponding agricultural activities.
The Trivulzio coat of arms, set inside a garland, is visible at the top: the emblem is of a siren breaking a file on a diamond, clearly alluding to the patron's indestructible solidity, as well as the motto "netes mai", the phonetic transliteration of *ne t'esmai* (never fear).
To the sides of the coat of arms are the sun and the sign of the zodiac. Coats of arms and monograms of the Trivulzio family frame the scenes.

An exceptional combination of the tapestry technique, mainly used across the Alps, and a Renaissance spatial setting in Italian taste, the twelve tapestries follow the solar cycle, starting with March and ending with February.
The tapestry for the month of *September* (d) portrays the couple and patrons Gian Giacomo Trivulzio and Beatrice d'Avalos, who seem to be gazing at the viewer, inviting him or her to join in. The tapestry for *August* (e) instead features the portrait of a great Renaissance artist, Donato Bramante, seated at a table to the left of the personification of the month.
The fresco in the Treasury Hall on the ground floor of the Castellana Tower, in the Rocchetta, is also by the great Milanese Renaissance painter Bramantino.

*above
and on opposite page*
Benedetto da Milano to a drawing by Bartolomeo Suardi called Bramantino, tapestries with the representation of *September* (d) and *August* (e), 1504-1509

8. The Museum of Archaeology
The Prehistory and Protohistory Section

On display in the Corte Ducale, in a room located below the Sforza apartments, is a selection of prehistoric and protohistoric finds most of which are from Lombardy. Arranged chronologically these objects range from the Neolithic period to the Roman colonization. Chipped and polished stone implements dating from the 6th to the 4th millennium BC, pottery, weaving and spinning tools illustrate the major technological innovations that characterized the whole of the Neolithic period, when society moved from being nomadic to sedentary. Several display cases are dedicated to the Bronze Age (in Northern Italy, 2200-900 BC), characterized by the working of copper and its alloys and by the use of the plough and cart. A choice of artefacts – funerary urns, armillae, pins, fibulas, and pendants – from the tombs of the Protogolasecca Culture, discovered in the Novarese and Milanese areas, bear witness to the passage from the Late Bronze Age (12th-10th centuries BC) to the Iron Age (9th-4th centuries BC). The grave goods found in some of the tombs typify the Golasecca Culture, prevalently known for the funerary objects found in the Golasecca-Sesto Calende-Castelletto Ticino, Como and Bellinzona areas. When the Gauls invaded in the early 4th century BC the Golasecca Culture declined. The Po Valley and Sub-Alpine regions underwent radical changes and the major towns were abandoned in favour of the Pre-Alpine and Alpine areas. The presence of the Gauls, with the flourishing of La Tène Culture in Italy, and the Romanization process of the territories are documented by the Roman armillae, swords, and pottery on view in the display cabinet that completes this part of the museum.

The History
The prehistoric and protohistoric collections formed in the 19th century were first officially housed in the Museo Patrio di Archeologia in Brera in 1862: the mission of the museum was to collect works and documents from all ages, from Prehistory to Modern times. Thereafter, in 1900, all the archaeological material was transferred to the new Museo Civico in the Sforza Castle. In the mid-1960s the Greek, Etruscan, and Roman collections were transferred to the new Museum of Archaeology set up in the former convent of San Maurizio, in corso Magenta, while the Egyptian and palaeo-ethnological collections remained in the Castle. The artefacts were eventually organized chronologically in the underground area of the Rocchetta in the 1970s. In 2003 they were displayed in the underground rooms of the Corte Ducale, where they can still be seen today.

8. Must-see

in the Museum of Archaeology
The Prehistory and Protohistory Section

a. First Tomb of the Warrior, Sesto Calende (Varese), late 7th century BC

Found inside the tomb, accidentally discovered by a farmer while ploughing his land in March 1867, is a precious collection of grave goods belonging to a person of high rank in the Golasecca district: parts of a cart, including the iron wheel rims fastened to the wooden wheels, horse bits and tack, a bronze helmet, and a pair of anatomically shaped bronze greaves, probably imported from Etruria.

The tomb also contained a short iron sword, as well as parts of its wooden sheath covered in bronze lamina, and a spearpoint also made of iron that must have been some two metres long. The grave goods also included a bronze lamina situla embossed with figured motifs, pottery, and the fragments of a funerary urn.

b. Tomb X, Albate (Como), mid-6th century BC

Tomb X of Albate presents the richest group of grave goods of the entire necropolis, and bears witness to the homage paid to the socially high-ranking deceased in the mid-6th

century BC. Definitely belonging to a woman, the grave goods include bronze, coral, and glass ornaments and some particularly elegant objects, such as a bronze lamina situla and a duck-shaped vase.

c. Tomb of the Situla, Trezzo sull'Adda (Milan), second half of the 6th-early 5th centuries BC

Discovered in 1848 in Trezzo sull'Adda, these grave goods included very valuable objects, both male and female.

Among the objects unearthed is a bronze lamina situla, decorated with a frieze featuring chasing scenes depicting dogs, deer, and fawns recalling the hunting theme. This artefact, made by skilled local craftsmen, is part of the production that characterizes the early Iron Age in Northern Italy and in the Central-Eastern Alpine area.

9. The Museum of Archaeology
The Egyptian Section

The Egyptian Section of the Museum of Archaeology located on the basement floor of the Corte Ducale features a thematic display, which allows the visitor to discover ancient Egyptian society. Representations on papyrus and artefacts, for example spinning and weaving implements, reveal some of the activities the Egyptians were involved in. Writing and support instruments such as the *ostraka* (terracotta fragments), wood and papyri show how the Ancient Egyptians wrote, and the three types of writing they used. Religious life and funerary worship are documented by numerous objects meant to ease the life of the deceased in the hereafter: amulets, mummiform figurines (*ushabty*), canopic jars and some examples of the so-called *Book of the Dead*. Also on view are both anthropomorphic and box-like sarcophagi, made from painted wood, as well as a mummy. The museum houses donated and acquired material, as well as a group of finds from the excavation campaigns – in part funded by the museum – carried out from 1934 to 1939 by Achille Vogliano, professor of papyrology of the Regia Università di Milano. Vogliano was one of the first papyrologists to undertake research in the field, attributing great importance to the archaeological context and recording everything that was found in a notebook. In Fayum he excavated several areas of the ancient settlement of Tebtynis and in the sacred area of Medînet Mâdi, at the centre of which he unearthed a temple founded in the Middle Kingdom and enlarged in the Ptolemaic era. Among the three hundred archaeological finds what particularly stands out is the statue of the founder of the temple of Medînet Mâdi, the Pharaoh Amenemhat III.

The History
A few of the objects donated in the early 19th century by the French Consul in Egypt Bernardino Drovetti and by the Austrian Consul Giuseppe Acerbi make up the start of the Egyptian collection. During the 19th century the initial nucleus was added to by numerous bequests. Between the 1930s and the 1940s the collection was enriched with material from the excavations in Fayum. In the Second World War the museum was dismantled and the materials stored for safekeeping. The finds were again exhibited in 1973, thanks to the director of the Civiche Raccolte Archeologiche, Gian Guido Belloni, in the basement of the Rocchetta. In 2003 the collection was re-installed in the basement of the Corte Ducale, where it is located today. Donations and acquisitions have further enhanced the Milanese collection, which today numbers about three thousand finds.

e.

9. Must-see

in the Museum of Archaeology
The Egyptian Section

d. *Statue of Amenemhat III*, **limestone, Middle Kingdom, XII dynasty (ca. 1853-1805 BC), from Medînet Mâdi, A. Vogliano excavations, 1936-1937**
Between 1936 and 1937 during the excavation campaigns in Medînet Mâdi, Fayum, led by papyrologist Achille Vogliano, the statue of Amenemhat III, pharaoh of the XII dynasty, came to light amidst the remains of a temple. The temple, founded by the sovereign himself, was dedicated to Renenutet, snake goddess of the harvest, to Sobek, crocodile god and patron of the region, and to Horus, falcon god. The pharaoh is portrayed seated on a cubical trunk with the uraeus on his forehead, symbolizing royalty; on his knees is a tray for offerings. Legible on either side of his legs are the names of the sovereign with the epithet "beloved by Renenutet of Gia", Medînet Mâdi's Egyptian name.

e. *The Sarcophaguses of Peftjauauyaset*, **stuccoed and painted cedarwood, Late Period, XXVI dynasty (7th century BC), from Thebes**
This anthropoid sarcophagus, which had belonged to Peftjauauyaset, shows considerable artistic quality, owing to the refined style of the face and decorations. On the outside of the lid is Nut, the winged goddess of the sky holding the breath of life (*ankh*), kneeling between her two sisters, the goddesses Isis and Nephthys. Carved below Nut is a vertical band of hieroglyphics, at one time filled with coloured glass paste, bearing Peftjauauyaset's name. The funerary rite to protect the deceased after death (the so-called "hourly wakes") is painted inside the alveus. The formulae are in cursive hieroglyphs around the goddess of the sky Nut, stretched in an arc shape like the heavenly vault. All that remains of the coffin that contained the sarcophagus is the lower part, its outer surface painted with funeral deities.

f. *Block Statue of a Dignitary*, **light green breccia, III Intermediate Period (1070-655 BC), provenance unknown**
The block statue, so-called owing to its geometric form, reproduces a figure crouching with its knees up pulled against its chest and wrapped in a tunic, on which the free-standing head emerges. The hands are carved on the horizontal surface. On the frontal side is an inscription, unfortunately incomplete, that bears the formula of the offering, in which the statue's patron, unknown as his name is no

longer legible, invokes the goddess Hathor. Owing to the stylistic rendering of the wig and the facial features it is believed that the sculpture was made in the III Intermediate Period, perhaps during the XXV dynasty (746-655 BC), a time when this type of statue was particularly widespread.

g. *Imhotep*, bronze, Late Age, XXVI dynasty (664- 525 BC), provenance unknown

This statuette represents Imhotep, Prime Minister of King Djoser (III dynasty, 2630-2611 BC) and a talented architect.

He is credited with the invention of a new type of tomb, entirely made of stone and featuring steps, built in the necropolis of Saqqara. The type of burial conceived by Imhotep constitutes an intermediate passage between the previous tombs known as "Mastaba" and the famous pyramids. The papyrus spread on the architect's legs tells us he is a protector of scribes.

h. *Models for Sculptors*, limestone, early Ptolemaic Period (4th-3rd century BC), provenance unknown

The refined portraits on limestone slabs exhibited in the museum are models that Egyptian sculptors used to make reliefs or teach art. The use of these models was already known from the New Kingdom (16th-12th centuries BC), but it became more widespread in the Late and Ptolemaic Periods (7th-1st centuries BC). One object shows the profile of a sovereign wearing a crown adorned with the uraeus, the snake symbolizing royalty. Another slab, used on both sides, shows a young sovereign wearing a wig with the uraeus on the front and a wide necklace, barely outlined. Illustrated on the back is a female face with a headdress in the vulture shape, both a divine and royal attribute. The stylistic rendering, the rounded face and the thick lips that wrinkle upwards in the carved figures are proof of its late date, probably the early Ptolemaic period, notwithstanding the fact that they were made according to earlier canons, with the head in profile, and the eye and shoulder shown frontally.

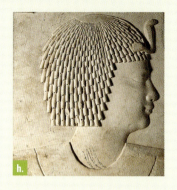

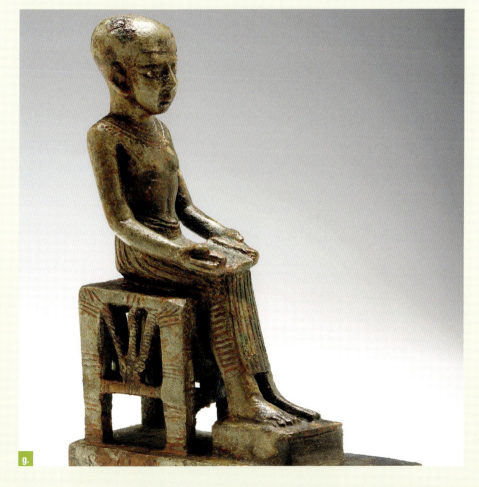

The Cultural Institutes of the Sforza Castle

A place of culture as well as art, the Castle is host to some of the major cultural institutions related to Milan, Italy, and the rest of the world. With their huge holdings they bear witness to the collecting passions of many illustrious citizens and their ambition to convey historical and artistic memories to the city of Milan.

Archivio Storico Civico e Biblioteca Trivulziana
Established in 1935 when the Trivulzio collection was annexed to the pre-existing Historical Archive of Milan, the institute currently owns over one thousand three hundred manuscripts, one thousand three hundred incunabula, sixteen thousand *cinquecentine*, as well as one hundred eighty thousand printed editions. Leonardo da Vinci's remarkable *Libretto di appunti* (Notebook) is among the manuscripts preserved. The archive holds the documents for the City of Milan and the Duchy from 1385, and the documents of the city administration until around 1927, in addition to the private archival fonds acquired over time.

Civica Raccolta delle Stampe "Achille Bertarelli"
Dedicated to the Milanese collector Achille Bertarelli (1863-1938), who in 1925 donated his collection of more than three hundred thousand prints to the City of Milan, the institute houses more than a million works, including about fifteen thousand artistic prints, from the first woodcut proofs of the 15th century to contemporary prints, organized iconographically. The wealth of material is divided into themed sections: plants and views, historical, artistic, and popular prints, advertising art, publishing art, design art, bookplates, fashion figurines, fans, games and playing cards, calling and greeting cards, coloured papers, postcards, almanacs and calendars, illustrated writing paper, currency and securities, food lists, heraldry, and flags. Added to this exceptional assortment of materials, which makes the Bertarelli a treasure trove for scholars and enthusiasts alike, is a collection of antique books and a choice of modern texts.

Civico Archivio Fotografico
The Photographic Archive, founded in 1933 thanks to the architect Luca Beltrami's passion for photography, is now one of the most important Italian institutes devoted to the conservation of photographic heritage. Gathered here are eight hundred fifty thousand original photographs, from 1840 to our day, documenting not just the evolution in printing techniques, but also the historical events, social life, artistic heritage, and journeys of a distant past. The most important fonds include the photo collections of Beltrami and of Lamberto Vitali, an art historian and the pioneering scholar and collector of Italian photography.

Civico Gabinetto Numismatico e Medagliere
The Gabinetto Numismatico e Medagliere was established in 1919, headquartered in the Castle, from the merger between two important coin and medal collections, the former the property of the City of Milan, the latter of the State. Today it preserves a significant collection of about two hundred eighty thousand items including coins and medals, ranging from the archaic output of the mints of Asia Minor (6th century BC) down to the Italian and European coins minted in the modern and contemporary ages.

opposite page
Marcello Dudovich,
Mele-Children's Clothing,
Naples, 1906, poster,
Civica Raccolta delle
Stampe "Achille Bertarelli"

below
Journal des dames et des modes, Biblioteca d'Arte, Emeroteca

Civico Gabinetto dei Disegni
Located in the Castle since 1972, the institute holds the drawings from the municipal collections since 1862. Today it houses about twenty-eight thousand prints from the 14th to the 20th centuries: these include the independent plans and exercises of Italian and foreign schools in a wide range of techniques and themes used for figurative drawing, architecture, and ornamentation.

CASVA, Centro di Alti Studi sulle Arti Visive
A cultural institute of the City of Milan established in 1999, the CASVA, active since 2002, is situated in the Castle and has gradually become the "mother of all archives" of the architects who have mainly worked on Lombard soil. It is a centre for studies inherent to architecture, design, graphic arts, figurative and visual arts.

Biblioteca d'Arte
With its holdings of over one hundred thousand volumes devoted to the arts, applied arts, museum studies, graphic art, architecture, design, fashion, it is one of the most important Italian institutes specialized in the artistic sector. It also includes a core of rare editions, among which an important series of in-folio art atlases from the 17th-19th centuries, an antique fond made up of thousands of editions from the 16th to the 19th centuries, and the especially interesting special fond of *Cartelle e Libri d'artista*, with originals from Treccani to Fiume, from Kandinsky to De Chirico, from Pomodoro to Depero. The one thousand six hundred art publications in the library (of which two hundred eighty-six are current) and the series collections can be consulted in the off-site periodicals library.

Biblioteca Archeologica e Numismatica
Established in 1808 thanks to the merger between the library and archive collections of the Numismatic Gabinetto of Brera and the Museo Patrio di Archeologia, the library was moved to the Castle after 18 May 1916. Today it boasts a bibliographic holdings of about thirty-five thousand items, including one thousand one hundred twenty-five antique editions. Also present are repertories and digital collections, as well as numerous fonds, protocols, letters and registers.

Ente Raccolta Vinciana
Established in 1905 thanks to Luca Beltrami's belief in the need to create a collection of Leonardo materials, in 1955 it was acknowledged by the State as "Ente morale." It is the major library dedicated to Leonardo da Vinci, housing some five thousand volumes published around the world.

The Parco Sempione

Extending to the north of the Castle is the Parco Sempione, realized between 1890 and 1893, in the forms that are still recognizable today, by the architect Emilio Alemagna, who designed a vast English-style garden, with slight artificial mounds, clusters of trees reminiscent of the open countryside, waterways, and broad lanes for carriages.

As early as in the days of Gian Galeazzo Visconti, in the late 14th century, north of the recently built Castle a vast area was created, in part cultivated and in part to be used as a garden.

Francesco Sforza and his heirs had the Visconti park transformed, from 1457 onwards, into a genuine hunting park, the "barcho", populated by roe deer, deer, hares, pheasants, and partridges, brought to Milan from the Varese, the Seprio, and Lake Como.

This veritable hunting ground was flanked by part of a garden endowed with a fish farm and large agricultural areas, where wheat, millet, rye, and oats were grown. There was also an orchard.

Towards the end of the 15th century, during the rule of Ludovico il Moro, the ceremonies and feasting in the sumptuous ducal park boasted an architect of the caliber of Leonardo da Vinci. After the fall of the Sforza and the arrival of the subsequent dominations, the vast area fell into abandon and was set up as a parade ground for the foreign legions.

The Monuments

Beyond the Barcho Gate on the northern side of the Castle, as one enters the park, several structures and monuments are visible.

Mermaid Bridge

Dedicated to the Austrian Emperor Ferdinand I, this bridge was inaugurated in 1842 by the Archduke Ranieri, viceroy of Lombardy-Veneto.

The first metallic bridge in Italy, it was designed by the engineer Francesco Tettamanzi, cast by the Rubini-Scalini-Falck company in the foundry of Dongo, on Lake Como, and used as a walkway on the San Damiano canal (now Via Visconti di Modrone).

The four sensuous mermaids were very much to the liking of the Milanese, evoking fantasies and urban legends. Affectionately called the "Ghisini sisters", they became a rendezvous for couples and a place where university students would play pranks.

In 1930, after the inner canal was covered, the

right
Mermaid Bridge

below
Monument to Napoleon III

THE PARCO SEMPIONE

opposite page
Arman, *Musical Accumulation and Seating*

right
Giorgio De Chirico, *Mysterious Baths* Fountain

bridge was shortened and moved to the Parco Sempione.

Musical Accumulation and Seating

Created by the French artist Armand Pierre Fernandez, known as Arman (1928-2005), the composition presents the cement podium used by an orchestra director from which trumpets and other musical instruments flourish, while surfacing up from the tiers of the orchestra pit, as if entrapped in the cement, are iron chairs of different shapes.

The work was exhibited in the Parco Sempione, together with eleven other works, in 1973, on the occasion of the 15th Milan Triennial.

Monument to Napoleon III

In 1873 Francesco Barzaghi was commissioned to make a monument celebrating Napoleon III and the French troops that freed Milan from the Austrians, triumphantly entering the city on 8 June 1859.

In addition to the general project, the sculptor is also the author of the statue of the emperor on horseback. Antonio Bezzola made the bas-reliefs on the sides, portraying the death of General Espinasse in Magenta and the entrance of Napoleon III and Victor Emanuel II in Milan. Laurel wreaths on the sides of the basement recall the French commanders who fell during the assault, while inscriptions list the names of the two thousand five hundred eight-four soldiers and officers who lost their lives. Completed in 1866, the work was inaugurated in the park on 27 February 1927.

Mysterious Baths Fountain

Installed in the park in 1973, the fountain is Giorgio De Chirico's (1888-1978) largest sculpture, now in the Triennale Garden.

The complex, made of Vicenza stone, comprises eight elements set in a large tub with an undulating shape. A part of the bottom of the tub, ochre yellow in colour, recalls the waves in a wooden floor pattern. It was precisely a wooden floor, so shiny that it reflected the legs of the people walking on it, that inspired the artist to create a parallel between the floor and the water and the design for this fountain. On the occasion of the restoration ending in 2010, the two swimmers and fish were replaced with copies. The originals are now on display at the Museo del Novecento, in Milan. In 2015 further work restored the fountain's original bright colours.

Continuous Theatre

Designed by Alberto Burri (1915-1995), the theatre was placed in the Parco Sempione on the occasion of the 15th Milan Triennial.

The artist set an open stage in the urban space, formed by a base and six tons of steel 6 metres high, painted white on one side and black on the other.

Dismantled and destroyed in 1989, Burri's theatre was rebuilt in 2015 thanks to the contribution of Alberto Toffoletto, to celebrate the centennial of the artist's birth and the opening of EXPO.

opposite page
Giorgio De Chirico, *Mysterious Baths* Fountain, detail of a swimmer (copy)

below
Alberto Burri, *Continuous Theatre*

following page
Leonardo da Vinci? (1452-1512), *Head of Leda*, red chalk on red-prepared paper, Milan, Civico Gabinetto dei Disegni

Essential References

G. Agosti, J. Stoppa, *I mesi del Bramantino*, Milan 2012.

P. Allevi, *Museo d'Arti Applicate. Armi da fuoco*, Milan 1990.

Il Castello Sforzesco di Milano, edited by M.T. Fiorio, Milan 2005.

C. Catturini, *La Sala delle Asse di Luca Beltrami: alcune novità documentarie sull'attività di Ernesto Rusca decoratore e restauratore, con qualche nota sull'allestimento di questo ambiente nella prima metà del Novecento*, in "Rassegna di Studi e di Notizie", XXXVI, 2013, pp. 63-76.

C. Catturini, *Leonardo da Vinci nel Castello Sforzesco di Milano: una citazione di Luca Pacioli per la "Sala delle Asse" ovvero la "camera dei moroni"*, in "Prospettiva", 147-148, July-October 2012, pp. 159-166.

S. Ceruti, *L'antico Egitto nel Castello Sforzesco di Milano. Opere scelte dalle Civiche Raccolte Archeologiche*, Comune di Milano 2010.

Dagli Sforza al design, sei secoli di storia del mobile. Il Museo delle Arti Decorative del Castello Sforzesco, edited by C. Salsi, Cinisello Balsamo 2004.

Luca Beltrami. 1854-1933 Storia, arte e architettura a Milano, edited by S. Paoli, Cinisello Balsamo 2014.

Eugenio e Mario Quarti nelle raccolte del Castello Sforzesco, edited by F. Tasso, Milan 2008.

Maestri della scultura in legno nel Ducato degli Sforza, edited by G. Romano, C. Salsi, Cinisello Balsamo 2005.

L. Melegati, *Le porcellane europee al Castello Sforzesco*, Milan 1999.

Michelangelo. La Pietà Rondanini nell'Ospedale Spagnolo nel Castello Sforzesco, edited by C. Salsi, Milan 2015.

Il mobile italiano nelle collezioni del Castello Sforzesco a Milano, edited by C. Salsi, Milan 2006.

G. Mori, *La collezione dei vetri artistici*, Milan 1996.

Museo d'Arte Antica del Castello Sforzesco. Pinacoteca, edited by M.T. Fiorio, tome I-V, Milan 1997.

Museo d'Arte Antica del Castello Sforzesco. Scultura lapidea, tome I, II, III, IV, Milan 2012-2015.

Museo di Arti Applicate. Le ceramiche, vols. 1-3, Milan 2000-2002.

Museo degli Strumenti Musicali, edited by A. Gatti, Milan 1998.

Museo degli Strumenti Musicali del Castello Sforzesco a Milano, edited by A. Restelli, Milan 2014.

M. Palazzo, *Il disegno preparatorio della pittura murale della Sala delle Asse. Alcune note sul suo rinvenimento a fine Ottocento*, in "Rassegna di Studi e di Notizie", XXXVII, 2014-2015, pp. 13-32.

S. Paoli, *Il Civico Archivio Fotografico di Milano. Note per una storia dell'Istituto e delle sue collezioni*, in "AFT. Rivista di Storia e Fotografia. Semestrale dell'Archivio Fotografico Toscano", XXII, 2006, no. 43 (June), pp. 3-4.

S. Paoli, *La Sala delle Asse. Fotografia e memoria fra le trame di un archivio*, in "Rassegna di Studi e di Notizie", XXXVI, 2013, pp. 207-224.

La Pietà Rondanini: il Michelangelo di Milano. Conoscenza e conservazione, edited by M.T. Fiorio, L. Toniolo, Milan 2006.

La Pinacoteca del Castello, edited by M.T. Fiorio, M. Garberi, Milan 1987.

La Pinacoteca del Castello Sforzesco a Milano, edited by L. Basso, M. Natale, Milan 2005.

C. Salsi, *Michelangelo. La Pietà Rondanini nell'Ospedale Spagnolo nel Castello Sforzesco*, Milan 2014.

La Raccolta Bertarelli - DVD, edited by Giovanna Mori, Milan 2008.

La Raccolta Bertarelli e la Grafica, edited by C. Salsi, exhibition catalogue, Milan 2009.

La scultura al Museo d'Arte Antica del Castello Sforzesco a Milano, edited by M. T. Fiorio, G. Vergani, Milan 2010.

Lo Studio di Fonologia. un diario musicale 1954-1983, edited by M.M. Novati, Milan 2009.

Terrecotte nel Ducato di Milano. Artisti e cantieri del primo Rinascimento, edited by M.G. Albertini Ottolenghi, L. Basso, Milan 2011.

T. Tomba, G. Brusa, *Museo d'Arti Applicate. Strumenti scientifici-Orologi*, Milan 1983.

O. Zastrow, *Museo di Arti Applicate. Oreficerie*, Milan 1993.

Photolithography
Studio Fasoli s.r.l., Verona
Printing
L.E.G.O. spa, Vicenza
for Marsilio Editori® s.p.a. in Venice

Xeroxed copies for the reader's personal use may equal 15% of each volume/ issue upon payment to SIAE of the amount specified in art. 68, commas 4 and 5, according to law 22 April 1941 no. 633. Xeroxed copies for professional, economic, commercial or reasons other than personal must first be authorized in writing by CLEARedi, Centro Licenze e Autorizzazioni per le Riproduzioni Editoriali, Corso di Porta Romana 108, 20122 Milan, e-mail autorizzazioni@clearedi.org and website www.clearedi.org

EDITION										YEAR				
10	9	8	7	6	5	4	3	2	1	2016	2017	2018	2019	2020